DECODING

THE

MARKETPLACE

By

Alan Louis, PhD

Copyright Number: TX 8-392-741

Trademark Number: 87/654,321

ISBN eBook: 978-1-970479-75-1

ISBN Paperback: 978-1-970479-76-8

ISBN Hardcover: 978-1-970479-77-5

To my dear wife, Almie.

About the Author

Alan Louis brings 37 years of experience in the marketplace, drawing on his Christian faith which has shaped his distinctive perspective on the intersection of business and Scripture. With a career spanning multiple continents, Alan has honed his expertise in decoding the complex systems that govern commerce. Shaped by both trials and triumphs, his journey has cultivated a deep understanding of holistic marketplace dynamics - enabling strategic alignment while highlighting Scriptural principles that guide wise marketplace engagement.

As the author of Decoding the Marketplace, Alan draws from his global experience, including his role in a multi-generational family business grounded in an extensive background in church life, sports, and academia, culminating in a PhD. His book is not just a guide to understanding marketplace systems but a call to align these practices with covenantal values rooted in Scripture. Alan's insights are deeply informed by his faith, which he sees as the ultimate decoder of the marketplace's hidden codes.

Beyond his professional life, Alan is a dedicated family man and a lifelong learner, always seeking fresh revelations of faith to guide his work and personal journey. His commitment to the "business of family" underscores his belief in the extraordinary power of grace in business affairs. Through personal anecdotes and hard-earned wisdom, Alan invites readers to join him on this journey of discovery and transformation, where the marketplace becomes a space not just for profit, but for purpose and grace.

For more information on the Book & Author, refer to www.decoding.market

In Gratitude Along the Path of Faith

A subject on grace must overflow with gratitude, so I offer heartfelt thanks as follows, reflecting Christ's grace to me:

To my Heavenly Father, my Lord Jesus Christ, and the Holy Spirit my Helper.

To my dear wife of 30 years, Almie, God's precious gift, chosen by His hand, the flame of my heart, bearing His love.

To my dear children, Colia, Calvyn, Ame & Anneke, where my testimony rests, each one a fortress round my heart.

To my dear parents, Dad and Mom, who first taught me to kneel, and helped me discover life's true worth in Christ.

To my four brothers, watchful and wise, and to teachers and ministers of the sacred Word.

To friends across many lands whose care came freely given, who sowed generously, a glimpse of heaven.

To the guides of thought at my school and university, rich in weight, and Bible study friends across many nations.

To prayer intercessors, quiet and unseen, and literary mentors, known only through their words.

To those who lent their hearts and skill to shape and market this book, and to my faithful work colleagues.

TABLE OF CONTENTS

PREFACE

The vivid photograph of a shooting star adorning this book's cover captures the essence of an atom splitting—a transformative act where smaller nuclei emerge, releasing radiant energy and light. Likewise, the shooting star symbolizes a dynamic shift, embodying hope and renewal. In the context of this book, it represents the reimagining of the marketplace: its core, much like an atom, can be thoughtfully broken down into smaller, uplifting practices. This process unleashes positive energy, fostering innovation, connection, and growth from within.

The decoding and codes presented here are not abstract theories, but practical insights for those prepared to look beyond the surface of everyday business activity.

This book, written on such a complex and sensitive topic, was not undertaken with the belief that I hold any special authority on the subject. Rather, I write prayerfully and with my best effort, not based on any presumption, but grounded in sincerity forged through my 37 years of marketplace experience, refinement, and a heartfelt journey of discovery. I have encountered many situations that are rare for others to experience.

What I believed to be my mind playing games on me with these codes, I have now played the game long enough to clearly see the truth and relevance of these codes. I therefore do not extend my thoughts with the weight of mere opinion, but with the clarity of deep insights and wounds, and mostly my faith in the Triune God Who reveals deep and mysterious things and knows what lies hidden in darkness.

The insights gained are not always immediate, and sometimes, they surface only after years of patient observation and prayerful alignment. A devoted businessperson does not permit himself/herself to be overcome by trials, because the individual prepares for them as a priority before climbing the mountain of success. If you are not aware of the existence of these codes (which are like a double-edged sword in your business life), how can you remotely attempt to climb to the top of Mount Everest? Decoding helps us to interpret that which we fail to comprehend or even to bring adequate language to our emotions and experiences. Only time can tell whether a decision or circumstance is profitable or detrimental to us at a certain moment, but decoding gives us both a head-start and a tremendous advantage.

Readers are encouraged not only to read but to pause, reflect, and examine their own business experiences in light of the codes shared here. The marketplace is, in many ways, a modern Game of Thrones. Most find themselves in deep pits of despair playing this game. The Bible asks the question: "For what will it profit you if you gain the whole world but forfeit your soul?" This book may greatly help you in your efforts to win this game, but more importantly to swerve it when it attempts to touch your soul. That's the very point of the detrimental marketplace codes; it aims to overreach to negatively affect your soul.

The purpose of this book is not an attempt to help you to perfectly understand every concept provided here, but rather to guide your discernment with the core message: much more is happening to you in the marketplace than meets the mind. So, may this book serve as a manual for clarity and courage as you journey through the winding paths, trials, and victories of the marketplace.

My journey required three University degrees before I completed a marketplace PhD, 37 years at our family business, and I operated in many countries. Though I long resisted the path of the pen which God gently guided me in a dream in 1999 just before the birth of my first child, the seed of my travailing prayer was only planted much later by the waters of Lake Zurich (Switzerland). In Shakespeare's own Stratford-upon-Avon (England), fifteen years shaped my literary voice, a voice I silenced but tried to recover for a few years in Singapore (Asia), choosing thereafter the long fast of waiting in the stillness of Stellenbosch's (South Africa) sun-soaked winelands. But destiny is patient. I took up the pen once more, and in Paris (France) - the city of my grandmother's roots - I unearthed the final threads, the hidden code that would unravel the marketplace's intricate maze.

In writing this book, my goal was to approach code as 'stealth' - which I term "code-as-stealth." The effectiveness of stealth technology lies in the meticulous coordination of components and aerodynamic principles. A single wing - like a standalone paragraph - or even a wing and a tail - a paragraph plus a chapter – does not make a stealth aircraft. True stealth comes from the integration of all components, perfectly aligned in the correct sequence and position. It's that meticulous attention to sequencing and positioning in narration, which are my efforts in the application of stealth, that assists to create the thrust in the code and the decoding.

Mastery in writing is elusive, yet we can still make every effort to code and decode with the best possible precision in comprehension, sequencing, and positioning, with code-as-stealth that is correct, meticulous, efficient, and whispers to the strings of the heart. Giving our best is one attribute, but true transformation of the heart and mind can only occur through the power of the Holy Spirit - therefore my prayer is always focused on seeking the guidance of the Helper.

May the Holy Spirit help you as you read, and may these pages assist you in discovering what was previously hidden, interpret what felt confused, and prompt you to proceed with deeper discernment.

This book is written from a Christian perspective, with the Word as a lamp to my feet and a light to my path as the Bible is inspired, inerrant, and infallible.

Alan Louis

CHAPTER 1
INTRODUCTION

Before we comprehend the marketplace, we should return to the very beginning, where light itself was given form and order.

"Then God made two great lights: the greater light to rule the day, and the lesser light to rule the night. He made the stars also."

(Genesis 1:16)

The marketplace, etched deep by ruin's breath, echoes the clang of hands pulled apart. Yet, in God's design, the greater light (the sun) is set to rule the lesser (the moon) – an order that, when applied to the marketplace, calls traders of this tapestry to rise with resilience and pursue business success through creativity, instead of being influenced by harmful practices that pull them away from their purpose.

This book aims to decode the mechanics of the marketplace, to present positive codes, and to enrich it with the redemptive harmony of divine grace for a fruitful business journey.

A significant marketplace indicator of warning signs is high household debt as a percentage of Gross Domestic Product (GDP). Household debt weaves deeply through the marketplace's loom. The heavier the burden, the harsher the thread, as each strand of commerce tightens its grip, and those who carry the weight feel its pull most acutely.

Data derived in the 3rd quarter of 2025 from CEICdata.com (a global economic data platform that provides macroeconomic and industry data) speak of a serious problem, a world ensnared by choices of the past. Now calls the hour for deeper reflection, to probe the codes that led us to this breach. In our effort to understand the issues, this narrative adopts a different approach – emphasizing constructive suggestions for change rather than criticism.

Where a country's household debt-to-GDP ratio should safely be less than 30% of GDP, only a few countries fall in this bracket (approximate percentages provided below on current data from CEIC), just to name a few (the following countries are not the only countries): Egypt (7.3%), Indonesia (10%), Turkey (10%), Uruguay (11%), Bolivia (11%), Philippines (11.7%), Albania (12%), Peru (16%), Mexico (17%), India (17%), Mauritius (20%), Botswana (21%), Morocco (23%), and Montenegro (26%).

However, most countries have a serious household debt-to-GDP problem. Consider these surprising figures (following countries are not the only countries): Malta (40%), South Africa (40%), Spain (49%), Germany (50%), Singapore (52%), USA (61%), China (63%), Japan (65%), France (74%), Cyprus (79%), UK (81%), Malaysia (84%), Thailand (89%), Norway (91%), Denmark (92%), Netherlands (94%), Canada (99%), South Korea (94%), UAE (106%), and Australia (116%).

Much like the well-known phrase during the USA space shuttle crisis: 'Houston, we have a problem,' a similar issue is unfolding here, necessitating the hour to decode. But before we begin to unearth the roots of economic, household, and personal imbalance, we must understand what exactly we are decoding.

Definition

In this book, the term *"code"* refers to any system of language, figures, or symbols used to represent everyday experiences in the marketplace. To *"decode"* is to convert those hidden messages into understandable, actionable truths.

This idea of decoding is central to navigating the marketplace. Rather than merely "interpreting" data or trends, we must learn to recognize and decipher the embedded mathematical and symbolic languages that govern marketplace behavior.

Too often, we assume these languages are neutral – mere tools of trade – but they are deeply moral. Every algorithm carries the fingerprint of its maker's worldview. Every system amplifies certain values while suppressing others. To decode, then, is not just to understand—it is to question the ethics behind the structure and ask: who does this code serve?

Similar to a theatrical performance, where every gesture and line holds a deeper meaning, the marketplace is often a performance scripted in numbers, signals, and silent assumptions.

Evidence of Codes in Everyday Systems

Consider *credit scores* – a clear example of a code in modern commerce. These numerical constructs claim to measure financial trustworthiness but often go further, projecting a distorted version of a person's "worth" in economic terms. Banks, creditors, and landlords use these scores to evaluate risk, while individuals are judged, included, or excluded based on algorithms (i.e., codes) they didn't design and can't easily challenge.

In our own ten-decade family business, we've long rejected this system. For decades, we extended credit and leases without ever consulting a credit score, and still maintained a repayment rate above 90%. In our view, this so-called "objective" code is deeply flawed, and may I say 'sinful.' It elevates control over compassion and reinforces inequality under the guise of mathematical precision.

The advertising industry often relies on coded language, visual symbols, and color schemes to trigger emotional responses and influence consumer behavior. For instance, luxury brands employ minimalist designs and gold tones to signal exclusivity and affluence. So too, many e-commerce websites employ "dark patterns" – subtle design tactics embedded in code that steer users toward choices they might not otherwise make, such as enrolling in recurring payments or consenting to data tracking.

The Role of Mathematics In Coding

Mathematics sits at the heart of all commercial activity. Every contract, exchange, and valuation rests upon number logic – on how digits interact with meaning. The mathematical framework of the marketplace – rooted in models, algorithms, and optimization – often abstracts away human complexity in favor of efficiency, predictability, or profit.

High-frequency trading, a rarely discussed practice, relies on mathematical algorithms that execute trades within microseconds, exploiting patterns and fleeting arbitrage opportunities. These algorithms, however, are blind to long-term value, ethical concerns, and the broader social impact of market volatility. As a result, the human cost is significant: markets are becoming increasingly opaque and exclusive, distancing themselves from the needs and realities of everyday investors and the real economy.

We often forget that the systems we live by are shaped by the assumptions we make about value. It's, after all, a *number system*, not a *name system*. The *number system* is ruled by place value. For instance, the digit 9 in "19" carries less weight than the 9 in "191." In contrast, the name system, which reflects God's design, places value on *inherent character and relationships* rather than numerical position.

Name System: Dominated by Relationship

This stands in sharp contrast to the number system. Where numbers assign value based on external criteria, the name system treasures inherent worth – who you are, not what you own. Love, under this system, is not transactional. It is relational. It recognizes in others the values you've cultivated within yourself.

This is why slogans like "relationship-minded bank" often ring hollow. While banks serve a vital public function, their philosophies are rooted in numbers, not names. Their decisions are driven by ratios, risk models, and return forecasts – not empathy, trust, or spiritual discernment.

Only a *name system* can uphold the Golden Rule: *"Treat others the way you wish to be treated."* It is the system of covenant, of connection, and of God's design for true economy, i.e., the greater light is set to rule the lesser.

Love, when it's relational rather than transactional, is rooted in connection, empathy, and mutual presence, rather than in exchange, debt, or calculated gain. For example, a parent staying up all night to care for a sick child expects nothing in return, neither gratitude, nor money, or future compensation. The parental bond exists beyond reciprocity. The love affirms the child's intrinsic worth, not their utility.

Divine Codes in Scripture

Scripture itself affirms this design, not through spreadsheets, but through stories and names. Even the Bible affirms the primacy of names over numbers. As a child, I wondered why genealogies filled whole chapters of the Old Testament – until I realized names matter. Not just their meanings, but their relationships. They reveal lineage, identity, and the continuity of God's covenant across generations.

God's system is, and always has been, a *name system*. Isaiah 43:1 is a prime example: "I have called you by your name; You are Mine." God's relationship with individuals is therefore personal and covenantal, not statistical. And this truth invites us to reimagine the very metrics by which we measure worth. What if success were not defined by quarterly gains but by generational faithfulness? What if economic planning began not with interest rates, but with interdependence? These are not mere hypotheticals – they are spiritual recalibrations waiting to be lived. To be named is to be known and claimed in love.

The marketplace, as it currently exists, is different as it promotes a code of control. But Scripture calls us to *decode that system* – to realign ourselves with values that honor dignity, connection, and truth.

The Business of Family

At the heart of the marketplace – and at the heart of life itself – is *relationship*. The leadership thinker John Haggai, captured this beautifully when he observed, *"I don't know of anyone with serious money who hasn't a capacity for relationships – that's how integral friendship is to business"*[1] He went further to say that a network of friends is far more powerful than a mere network of acquaintances. It reaches deeper, lasts longer, and wields influence not through obligation but through trust and commitment.

This distinction between acquaintance and relationship is crucial, not only in leadership but in understanding the business of family – a concept far richer than simply being involved in a *family business*.

A *family business* typically refers to a company owned and operated by members of the same bloodline. Shareholding is inherited; loyalty is often assumed. I was born into such a setting, nearing six decades in the same business, where, as we like to say, *your share certificate is issued the day you are born.*

And yet, despite the nostalgic charm, family businesses have deep flaws. They are, like any other enterprise, made up of imperfect people making imperfect decisions. Being "family-owned" is no guarantee of relational depth or covenantal values. It can just as easily operate as any marketplace entity – transactional, competitive, and even divided.

But the *business of the family* is something else entirely. It is not about ownership. It is about *stewardship* of people, legacy, and divine purpose. This idea, which I describe as a *"family of families,"* speaks to an intentional weaving of relational bonds across households, generations, and even business partnerships. It places love, loyalty, and shared Godly values at the center, not control or inheritance. In essence, the business of family invests *"influence,"* whereas the marketplace codes encourage monetary investment.

In this vision, the business of family becomes a heart or even a ministry assignment. It's about building community, not just companies. It's about nurturing trust, not just net worth. This covenant-based approach to business is what gives families resilience across generations and what allows marketplace work to become hearts in motion.

Just as God builds His kingdom through names and relationships, we too are invited to build networks not of leverage, but from the heart. The marketplace may reward efficiency, but legacy rewards *"sincere heart motive."* In a world that often decodes people into metrics, the business of family dares to remember names.

The business of family, driven by heart not mind, is truly tested not around the comfort of a dinner table with friends, but in the harsh realities of the marketplace, where challenges are real and relentless. Our family business, albeit flawed like many others, has put this heart-in-motion to the test for over ten decades, building business relationships that have lasted for decades—a rare achievement.

The bottom line is this: a name system will beat a number system every time. Build your business on being relationally minded, and you will never regret that decision – "with all lowliness and gentleness, with longsuffering, bearing with one another in love."[2]

The important reason I strongly encourage the business of family is that the destructive codes are not tolerated.

The Code Dilemma

Marketplace codes are rarely spoken aloud, yet we feel them deeply. That heaviness you carry home after a draining day – the one that makes you mutter, *"Phooey, that was a bad day"* – is often the result of unseen forces working beneath the surface. These codes do not just affect our transactions; they target our very being.

To understand their impact, we must first consider the *tripart nature of humanity*: body, soul, and spirit. The *"body"* is our physical vessel, the *"soul"* houses our thoughts and emotions, and the *"spirit"* connects us to God. True well-being requires a balance among all three, but marketplace codes, especially deceptive or oppressive ones, often disrupt this harmony in subtle yet significant ways.

Psychologist Dr. Martha Beck offers a useful analogy in her research on the brain's relationship to anxiety and creativity. According to her studies,[3] the parts of the brain that process anxiety and creativity act like mirrors: when one is active, the other shuts down. So, when anxiety rises, creativity vanishes. Conversely, engaging in creative activity suppresses anxiety, allowing the brain to reset and breathe.

This toggle effect has a spiritual parallel. In my experience, unhealthy marketplace codes often disrupt not just our peace of mind but our spiritual rhythm. A banker advising you, *"You're not worth more credit,"* is not merely denying you a loan. They're delivering a coded message that strikes at your identity. And in that moment, your spirit is triggered, often without conscious awareness.

Instead of reacting with clarity or confidence, your spiritual channels – like prayer time – are silenced. Your internal connection to God is disrupted, not because you doubt Him, but because the emotional clutter of the code disorients your inner life.

This is the great dilemma of disruptive marketplace codes: they target your spirit, manipulate your soul, and only incidentally engage your mind. This is why even the most intellectually sound people can walk away from a boardroom or a banking desk feeling spiritually disoriented. Because the harm was never intellectual – it was spiritual. The code bypasses logic and invades the heart, whispering things like "You're not enough," or "You don't belong," until even prayer feels out of reach. That is why codes often leave us feeling uneasy, unsettled, and unsure of why.

Charles H. Spurgeon once said, "The law is for the self-righteous, to humble their pride; the gospel is for the lost, to remove their despair." In the spirit of this profound truth, I venture to expand it to include today's reality:

The law is for the self-righteous, to humble their pride; codes are for the unsuspecting, to catch them blind; the gospel is for the lost, to remove their despair.

When we fail to decode these forces, we risk becoming spiritually numb. But when we recognize the codes, we can resist the destructive ones. When we decode them, we reclaim clarity, dignity, and spiritual authority. The marketplace doesn't just trade in goods – it merchants in messages, many of which are meant to confuse or dethrone.

The reader Is encouraged not just to assemble knowledge of codes but to be resilient to negative codes. It's to rise above it by staying aligned with truth, creativity, destiny, and your relationship with God. Decoding, in this sense, becomes an act of the heart connecting with the soul – a form of spiritual clarity that returns your soul to peace and your spirit to purpose. This book is your invitation to decode the noise, to reclaim clarity, and to re-enter the marketplace with spirit-led purpose.

CHAPTER 2
THE MONEY ISSUE

"And my God shall supply all your need according to His riches in glory by Christ Jesus."

(Philippians 4:19)

Welcome to the marketplace, where wonders and woes in silence resound. Unravel the codes, let wisdom arise, and giants once looming will shrink to their size.

Before we can fully grasp the hidden marketplace codes that influence our daily business decisions, we must first understand the basic financial language that enables these codes to operate. While many readers may already be familiar with some of these terms, this section is designed to bridge the gap for those who aren't. My goal is to make these foundational ideas accessible so that no reader, regardless of their background in economics or math, feels excluded from the journey of decoding.

This section is written not just for professionals in finance or business but for anyone seeking clarity in a world that often shrouds truth in technical language. To break free from the spiritual entanglements that marketplace systems can impose, we must first be equipped with both knowledge and discernment. Understanding these mechanisms is one step toward reclaiming financial freedom and aligning with God's order.

If you're well-versed in economics or monetary theory, consider this Chapter a necessary brief review. If not, I encourage you to read carefully. What initially appears to be standard textbook material, actually presents the groundwork for spiritual awareness and marketplace liberation.

The Force that Moves

While God is the true force that sustains life, money is often the force that moves human nature. It governs economies, dictates choices, and influences even our sense of identity and security. Without it, we would return to a barter system - exchanging goods or services directly, with no common medium of value.

To understand how wealth is manipulated - sometimes subtly, sometimes deliberately - it's essential to understand how money functions. This is especially vital in a world where economic systems can be designed to transfer power from the unsuspecting to the elite.

There are two primary forms of money:

o   Commodity Money: This includes items that hold intrinsic value, such as gold, silver, or even items like copper, alcohol, or grains. They can be used directly or exchanged because of their inherent worth.

o   Fiat Money: Unlike commodities, fiat money has no intrinsic value. Its worth comes from a government decree. A dollar bill, for instance, is merely paper unless we agree it holds purchasing power. This type of money can be printed, manipulated, and inflated, which makes it a tool for both progress and control.

Banknotes were first issued in 7th-century China, though it was another 1,000 years before paper money was issued for public use in Europe by Sweden's Stockholms Banco in 1661.[4]

It was Benjamin Franklin, a founding president of the United States, who said: "If you would want to know the value of money, go and try to borrow some." In the same vein, Spike Milligan said, "Money can't buy friends, but you can get a better class of enemy." There is also some truth to the statement that I once heard that "money can't buy happiness; it can, however, rent it."

Money (in this sense, I refer to fiat money) is a token of trust. Paper notes and coins are worth only a fraction of the amount they denominate, which is why money must be backed up by people's trust, i.e., trust that the government will ensure the money is worth something in the future.

In essence, money is a commodity, nothing more. The Christian statesman John Haggai had this to say about money: "It has no intrinsic value. It can accomplish great good, and it can wreck lives. It all depends on how it's used."

One-Dimensional Living

If materialism is the driving motivation of your life, you will never be satisfied, no matter how much you earn or how much you acquire.

Throughout the Bible, Jesus warns against the transitional nature of riches and the anxiety we suffer when we make this our focus. His caution was against the dangers of materialism and the folly of one-dimensional living, which is both selfish and debasing of others.

It is not that money or possessions are wrong in themselves; it is the attitude we have toward them that is usually where the problem lies. As Oprah Winfrey, the talk show host, aptly commented, "Everyone wants to ride with you in the limo, but what you want is someone who will take the bus with you when the limo breaks down."

There is no doubt that the world is in financial turmoil, but we still have the freedom to choose how we should respond to it.

According to Franklin Roosevelt, the 32nd USA president, "The test of our progress is not whether we add more to the abundance of those who have much; it is whether we provide enough for those who have too little."

Oscar Wilde, the Irish writer and poet, noticed this tendency when he said: "There is only one class in the community that thinks more about money than the rich, and that is the poor."

The Masquerading Signs

In the journey of decoding the marketplace, two terms frequently surface that often masquerade as signs of success: *solvency* and *liquidity*. While they may sound technical, understanding them is crucial, not just for financial professionals but for anyone navigating the marketplace with wisdom and spiritual discernment.

'Solvency' refers to a company's ability to meet its long-term obligations. It asks: *If all debts were called in tomorrow, could the company's assets cover them?* Solvency speaks to long-term health and sustainability, namely, whether a business can weather storms or if it's just postponing collapse.

But solvency alone isn't enough. A business also needs 'liquidity' - the ability to meet short-term needs and unexpected demands. In other words, it's not just about having enough but having access to enough *now*.

Economists often joke that solvency is when you don't need to smooth your hair and straighten your tie before walking into the bank. Liquidity is when the bank smiles back and says, "Welcome."

Measuring the Financial Pulse

Solvency is typically measured using the 'current ratio' - the value of current assets divided by current liabilities. A healthy benchmark is a 2:1 ratio, meaning the business owns twice as many liquid assets as it owes in the short term. This margin accounts for the fact that converting assets into cash, especially quickly, often involves a loss.

When my family and I spent time in the beautiful town of Stratford-upon-Avon in England, locals would greet me warmly: "Hello, friend," charmed by my South African accent. But at the bank counter, it was "Hi, stranger." It eventually dawned on me - my liquidity was not speaking the same language as my accent.

Liquidity is about more than charm; it's about readiness. It reflects how easily a company can convert its assets - cash, investments, or inventory - into spendable money to meet immediate obligations. A high current ratio suggests strength in liquidity, while a low one is a red flag for potential short-term stress.

Two Crises in Contrast

It's important to distinguish between two types of financial crises:

- A *liquidity crisis* occurs when a company owns valuable assets but cannot access enough cash when needed - imagine trying to pay your electricity bill with a valuable painting you can't sell in time.

- A *solvency crisis*, on the other hand, arises when a company's liabilities outweigh its assets entirely. It's not just a matter of timing - it's a matter of being overextended beyond what one owns.

This distinction is critical not only for understanding financial health but also for navigating the spiritual dimension of stewardship. Sometimes, like companies, people appear solvent, owning homes, investments, and even titles. But when life's emergencies strike, the question becomes: *Are we liquid enough in cash and character to respond readily and correctly?*

Understanding Debt

Debt is the amount of money borrowed by one party from another. Companies and individuals use debt as a method for making purchases that they could not afford under normal circumstances. A debt arrangement gives the borrowing party permission to borrow money under the condition that it is to be paid back at a later pre-determined date, with interest (rarely without interest).

We need to heed Proverbs 22:7, "The borrower is servant to the lender." In the strategy of creditors or 'chieftains' to gain absolute control of their subjects, debt is the key weapon they use to enslave. This is the primary reason I introduced insights into global household debt in the opening chapter of this book.

If you start falling behind on your debts, you will find it extremely difficult to catch up because interest, late payment fees, legal notices, legal defenses, start escalating, and creditors are like sharks in that once they smell blood, they often go for the kill. Borrowing a phrase from Bob Sorge, who describes so well the torment of infirmity (or debt):

> *"It snakes its cords around the ... souls, and minds of its victims, sucks the life out of their spirits, and drags them into its dungeons of hopelessness, loneliness, grief, and depression. There they sit, languishing in their hovels, staring blankly at their screens, looking for any distraction that might anesthetize their suffering and boredom. [The people with high debt] exist, but they do not live."[5]*

The stress of debt can also lead to health problems and even mental problems, such as severe depression, anger, and family breakdown. One of the challenges we face is that we live in a world that is obsessed with material gain. Everywhere we look, we are encouraged to buy things that we do not need, with money that we do not have, to impress people that we do not know.

At the heart of many financial struggles - both personal and corporate - is the unspoken pressure to maintain a lifestyle we cannot afford. *Excess debt*, in its essence, is often driven by a desire to meet perceived standards of success, even when our resources fall short. It's not just a numbers problem; it's a reflection of deeper values, pressures, and unchecked expectations.

As we navigate the terrain of business and finance, we must ask: *What is our response to the growing debt crisis?* One thing is clear - if we simply follow the flow, conforming to what is culturally or commercially "normal," we risk losing our moral and relational footing. The downstream current is strong, but spiritual clarity calls us to swim against it.

We cannot examine the mechanics of money and banking without recognizing their lineage -*economics* and *mathematics*. These are the "parents" of our modern financial systems, and if we're to find answers to the flaws that plague money and debt, we must explore the wisdom - or warnings - embedded in these older disciplines.

This book is not written as an academic thesis. It is envisioned as a practical and spiritual guide for the everyday reader (business-minded but soul-conscious). While economics and mathematics can be dense fields, the next few pages will introduce their principles in hopefully a clear and approachable way.

These disciplines form the scaffolding of how the marketplace operates, and a basic understanding of them will serve as an important foundation for the rest of the journey. Skipping them would be like trying to decode a map without first learning its symbols.

Economics

As an academic, I mastered and took an active interest in economics. Economics is not all about money, but money makes economists of us all. In this regard, Edmund Conway, economics editor, aptly said, "Ask someone to pay the price for something as opposed to offering it for free, or for a favor and you'll flick an invisible switch inside them."[6]

At its heart, economics is the study of people. Conway also says, "Economics examines what drives human beings to do what they do and looks at how they react when faced with difficulties or successes. It investigates choices people make when given a limited set of options and how they trade them off against each other. It is a science that encompasses history, politics, psychology, and, yes, the odd equation or two. If it is history's job to tell us what mistakes we've made over the past, it is up to economics to work out how to do things differently next time around." [7]

Adam Smith, possibly the father of economics, believed that self-interest is good for society but was careful to distinguish between self-interest and pure, selfish greed. His theory was that it is in our self-interest to have a framework of laws and regulations that protect us, as consumers, from being treated unfairly. According to Smith, "It is not from the benevolence of the butcher, the brewer, or the baker that we expect our dinner, but from their regard to their own interest. We address ourselves, not to their humanity but to their self-love, and never talk to them of our own necessities but of their advantages."

Economics is the study of how the law of supply and demand affects human relationships. The way these two forces interact determines the value we place on goods and services. Alfred Marshall, Victorian economist who popularized supply-demand curves and tables, said something interesting: "We might as well reasonably dispute whether it is the upper or under the blade of a pair of scissors that cuts a piece of paper, as whether value is governed by demand or supply."

The ideological battle underlying modern economics may best be understood in the opposing economic doctrines of John Maynard Keynes[8] and Milton Friedman.[9] Keynes paid more attention to unemployment than inflation and warned that the economy could be improved by a certain amount of state interference. On the other hand, Friedman argued that people should be left to their own devices, with the government's main role being to monitor and control the amount of money flowing around the economy.

It is not within the scope of this book to consider the result of the clash between these two economic titans, but rather to propose an additional dimension to economic theory, which is the subject of the last chapters.

Although the Smith, Keynes, and Friedman economic theories have taught us much, they are not fail-safe, as the economics commentator Martin Wolf[10] observed shortly before the UK and the US dipped into recession: "Just as Keynes's ideas were tested to destruction in the 1950s, 1960s and 1970s, Milton Friedman's ideas might suffer a similar fate in the 1980s, 1990s and 2000s. All gods fail if one believes too much."

When deliberating on the best form of government or economics, on the far left, one would possibly find *Utopia,* and on the far right, *Capitalism*. A comparison between the two is worth considering.

Utopia versus Capitalism

Thomas More[11] coined the term 'Utopia,' which he saw as a humanist paradise, a pro-communist society in which everything is held in common, men and women live together harmoniously as equals, where religious and racial intolerance is banished, and education is provided by the state. Gold is valueless and used to make chamber pots.

For years, Utopians have blamed all society's ills on the inequities in wealth, which they assume causes greed, envy, and all manner of social unrest. As a remedy, they advocate leveling the playing field by implementing a system of egalitarian communism in its place.

It was Winston Churchill, British Prime Minister, who said that the inherent virtue of a communist system is the equal sharing of miseries, whereas the inherent vice of capitalism is the unequal sharing of blessings. Economist Adam Smith strongly advocated the idea that a free market was the most effective approach to managing the economy. His introduction of the ideals of classical capitalism speaks for itself because this system is naturally self-regulating, meaning variables like cost, price, supply, and demand originate and work within the system and need no external aid in order to allow the system to function as it should.

Advocates of capitalism stress its unparalleled capacity to generate economic growth. Unquestionably, the period of capitalism's dominance has coincided with a spectacular increase in economic output.

The point of this comparison is that both doctrines have inherent flaws, and the solution to an improved economic and financial system lies somewhere in between. Since this book addresses some of the flaws inherent in the capitalist system, we will consider a brief analysis of capitalism.

Briefly Examining Capitalism

Merriam-Webster defines *capitalism* as "an economic system characterized by private or corporate ownership of capital goods, by investments that are determined by private decision, and by prices, production, and the distribution of goods that are determined mainly by competition in a free market." A broader definition is given by *Investopedia* as:

> "*An economic system based on a free market, open competition, profit motive, and private ownership of the means of production. Capitalism encourages private investment and business, compared to a government-controlled economy. Investors in these private companies (i.e., shareholders) also own the firms and are known as capitalists.*"

In such a system, companies and individuals have the right to own and use wealth to make a profit and to sell and purchase labor for wages with partial government control. The function of regulating the economy is then achieved mainly through the operation of market forces, where prices and profit dictate where and how resources are used and allocated.

Capitalism has been the dominant economic system in most parts of the world for the last two centuries. Banks and financial institutions thrive in a capitalistic society. The fault line in the theory and practice of capitalism has always been the extent to which scrutiny, regulation, and intervention on the part of the state are compatible with the proper operation of the capitalist system.

Money not a Master

It is a sobering truth: *greed for money* remains one of the most powerful driving forces behind theft, corruption, violence, and even murder. From embezzlement and fraud to global warfare and systemic exploitation, the pursuit of wealth has repeatedly fueled the darkest chapters in human history.

Alongside religion, money and wealth have been among the most divisive and explosive elements in society. Time and again, revolutions have been sparked by the dispossessed - those demanding their share of prosperity from systems designed to enrich the few. In modern times, the insatiable hunger of multinational corporations and banking giants to maximize profits and appease shareholders have often pushed the world to the edge of financial collapse.

But the deeper danger lies not in money itself - it lies in what Scripture identifies with piercing accuracy: *"The love of money is a root of all kinds of evil."*[12]

Why does Scripture caution so clearly against the love of money? Because money has a deceptive power. It promises what we were meant to receive from God - security, identity, and provision, yet delivers only temporary illusions. The greater our attachment to money, the more vulnerable we become to misplaced trust and spiritual erosion.

This is not a theoretical risk. It's a spiritual reality: money, when loved too deeply, becomes a rival to God. As Jesus warned, *"No one can serve two masters... You cannot serve God and mammon."* [13] If our hearts are divided, our direction will be too.

And before long, we find ourselves worshipping the provision instead of the Provider.

It's easy to forget that God is the true source of what we need. When we believe wealth is self-generated or deserved, we slip into pride. When we believe it's all we need, we slip into idolatry.

As we continue to explore the deeper workings of the marketplace, we must keep this truth in clear focus: *money is a tool, not a master*. Its place must remain under divine wisdom and covenantal principles. The warning is clear - if we fail to confront the spiritual risks money brings, we will never fully decode the systems that bind us.

Having examined one "parent" of modern economics - human desire and spiritual imbalance - we now turn to the other foundational pillar: *mathematics*. Just as emotion drives action, calculation builds the systems through which that desire takes shape.

Understand the Role of Mathematics

Mathematics lies at the heart of finance as all the processes depend on an understanding of the ways numbers work, how they interact with reality, and how, in some cases, certain equations that would normally have a simple solution are never-ending.

If you possess a grasp of the underlying principles, you will be well-positioned to understand your creditors and bankers. Useful understandings include an awareness of the two impressive numbers in math – π (Pi) and *e* – as they have special and irrational properties that replicate the actions of people. The very imperfection of these two mathematical constants is a trait that you can use to your advantage.

π, or pi, is probably the most famous number in mathematics. The new kid on the block is *e* when compared with its rival π. And, of course, when we think of the most famous numbers in mathematics, we must also include 0 and 1.

An insight into game theory is also particularly useful as it provides a way of calculating the impact of decisions made. The beauty is that creditors or chieftains often lack these basic understandings, so they will proceed to negotiate along their standard pathway while you have the upper hand gained through flexibility, insight, and intellect.

Pi or π

An interesting notion, albeit a bit of an aside, is the intriguing concept of π, which is a mathematical constant and is the length of the outside of a circle (the circumference) divided by the length across its center (the diameter). Its value, the ratio of these two lengths, does not depend on the size of the circle. Whether the circle is big or small, π is indeed a mathematical constant. The circle is the natural habitat for π, but it occurs everywhere in mathematics and in places not remotely connected with the circle.

We can never know the exact value of π because it is an irrational number,[14] which means that it cannot be expressed exactly as a ratio of two integers (such as 22/7 or other fractions that are commonly used to approximate π); consequently, its decimal representation never ends and never settles into a permanent repeating pattern.

Mathematicians are continually fascinated by π, and throughout the ages, many have tried to calculate its value. In 1853, William Shanks claimed a value correct to 607 places. In 1949, π was calculated to an even more remarkable 2,037 decimal places. And if that wasn't impressive enough, with the aid of computers, by 2002, the value of π had been computed to a staggering 1,241,100,000,000 places, which, if written down, would circumvent the world nearly 62 times![15]

e

In the same way as π, the number e is another mathematical constant and is in play wherever there is a discussion of growth. Referring to any number of things, whether it be physical qualities, money, or populations, growth invariably involves e.

The number e is the approximate equivalent of 2.71828, which is the base of the natural logarithm. As it approaches infinity, it is the limit of $(1+1/n)n$, an expression used to help explain compound interest.[16]

The number *e* itself also has applications to probability theory, where it arises in a way not obviously related to exponential growth. Suppose that a gambler plays a slot machine that pays out with a probability of one in n and plays it n times. Then, for large n (such as a million), the probability that the gambler will lose every bet is (approximately) 1/e. For n = 20, it is already 1/2.72.

Like the constant π, *e* is irrational: it is not a ratio of integers, and it is transcendental: it is not a root of any non-zero polynomial with rational coefficients. The connections between π and e are fascinating. The values of *e*π and π*e* are close, but *e*π > π*e,* with the approximate values being *e*π = 23.14069 and π*e* = 22.45916.

Why I bring up π and *e*, just like the nature of humanity, is that it is not possible to fix their value. These irrational mathematical constants cannot be fixed, just as decoding is a constantly moving target. All we can attempt to do is forego attempts for perfect solutions and rather focus on the ingredients to our understanding and exposure to codes more palatable.

The Importance of Game Theory

Game theory is a fascinating branch of mathematics, and I believe that a brief introduction to this all-important subject will be useful for the reader. I will interpret this complex topic only in layman's terms.

Game theory is basically the study of 'games' and is most helpful for decoding. Games, in the mathematical sense, are described as strategic situations in which there are multiple participants, i.e., two or more. Furthermore, the outcome of the decision any one individual makes is dependent on that individual's decision and the decisions made by all the other participants. According to *Investopedia*: "Game theory attempts to look at the relationships between participants in a particular model and predict their optimal decisions."

Let's consider a simple example: The Game of Debt.

In the game of debt, we have two participants, Lender and Borrower, who are in dispute. They each have to make the decision just before going to court to either continue fighting over their differences (fights) or to throw in the towel (deviate) at the last minute. The possible results in game theory are as follows:

Lender	Borrower	Result
Fights	Fights	Proceed to Court
Fights	Deviates	Lender is happy he wins; Borrower is sad he loses
Deviates	Fights	Borrower is happy he wins; Lender is sad he loses
Deviates	Deviates	Both hav to compromise

Let's now re-organize the possible results into a matrix, called the 'pay-off matrix,' with some numbers to make it easier to analyze:

o Both deviate and having to compromise = 0 for both

36

- Both fighting and going to court = -2 for both

- One fighting and one deviating = 1 for the winner (fighter) and -1 for the loser (deviator)

		Lender	
		Deviate	Fight
Borrower	Deviate	0/0	-1/1
	Fight	1/-1	-2/-2

A Simple Analysis of the Game of Debt:

Let's see what we can learn about how the game will be played out. The first matter we consider is something called a 'best response.' Essentially, let's imagine that we are the Borrower (since we are sadly never the Banker), and we know what the Lender will do. How do we react?

If we know that the Lender will deviate, we need only look at the left column. We see that if we (Borrower) deviate, we get 0, but if we continue to fight, we get 1. So, the 'best response' is to fight.

On the other hand, if we know that the Lender will fight, we need only look at the right column. We see that if we deviate, we get -1, and if we continue to fight, we get -2. So, the 'best response' in this permutation is to deviate.

In this game, the Lender has similar 'best responses.'

A Nash Equilibrium

If you have seen the Oscar-winning movie 'A Beautiful Mind' with actor Russell Crowe, you may remember that it was all about the brilliant mathematician John Nash, after whom, in real life, a 'Nash Equilibrium' was named.

A *Nash Equilibrium* ('NE') is when all players play the best response. In the game of debt illustrated above, both players wanting to fight and not deviate is not an NE because at least one player would have preferred to deviate. Also, both players deciding to deviate is not NE because at least one player would have preferred to fight.

However, when one player fights and the other deviates, this is a NE because neither player can improve their outcome by changing their action. Another way of saying this is that both players are playing their 'best response.'

Now let's turn the focus away from how financial institutions make decisions based on numbers, risks, and outcomes that ultimately profit them and ask, "how do people make decisions about their money, business, and investments?"

Prospect Theory

Most people believe their daily decisions are made rationally. According to the *Business Dictionary*, rational decision-making is "a method for systematically selecting among possible choices, that is based on reason and facts. In a rational decision-making process, a business manager will often employ a series of analytical steps to review relevant facts, observations, and possible outcomes before choosing a particular course of action."

On the economic scene, the 'rational decisions' are known as 'utility maximization.' In this process, we attempt to think through the most likely outcomes (probability-wise) and the value (utility) of those outcomes. We then choose the best of our options, which is called *normative theory*.[17] But there is a major drawback with this approach: studies have shown that, in reality, people don't operate this way, especially when it comes to potential gains and losses. This is so because people tend to attach far more importance to the possibility of *loss* than of *gain*.

Kahneman and Tversky won the 2002 Nobel Prize in Economics for their work on prospect theory, which describes decisions between alternatives that involve risk, i.e., alternatives with uncertain outcomes where the probabilities are known. Kahneman was cited for discovering "how human judgment may take heuristic shortcuts that systematically depart from basic principles of probability."

According to *Investopedia*, prospect theory suggests that people look at gains and losses differently and, as such, will base decisions on perceived gains rather than on perceived losses. In other words, if a person is given two equal choices, one based on possible gains and the other on possible losses, he will choose the former.

Studies have shown that individuals are far more sensitive to loss than to gain, so much so that they frequently take serious risks simply to avoid losses. As a result, they will often unwisely sell shares when the stock market dips rather than hold onto the stock, knowing it will rebound over time.

To demonstrate prospect theory, let's say that one investor is offered the same mutual fund by two different financial advisors. The first one tells the investor that the mutual fund has had an average return of 7% over the past five years. The second tells the investor that the same mutual fund has had above-average returns over the past ten years but has declined in recent years. According to prospect theory, an individual is more likely to buy the mutual fund from the first advisor, who expressed the rate of return as an overall 7% gain rather than a combination of gains and losses.

When people are faced with a decision involving outcomes they see as basically identical, they set a reference point and view lower outcomes as losses and larger outcomes as gains. The asymmetry of the S-curve is indicative of Warren Buffett's finding that "losses gain twice the emotional response of gains." People are risk-averse in relation to gains, but will gamble to avoid losses. The subjective value of a large gain is not much greater than that of a small gain, so there is little incentive for people to gamble in order to try to increase the size of the gain.

When options offer potential gains, people overwhelmingly tend to avoid risks, but when losses are possible, they will take far greater risks than otherwise simply to minimize those losses. Across the board, without respect to background or age, investors would much prefer to minimize the misfortune of loss than maximize the joy of gain.

Irrational Investing Behaviors

For the most part, people act completely irrationally. This is the basic premise behind a theory of Finance that Professor Bing Han titled "Prospect Theory and Applications in Finance."[18]

According to Professor Han, prospect theory can be explained by the choices investors make involving either risk aversion or loss aversion. Risk aversion holds that investors are unwilling to accept risk without compensation and will even purchase insurance to avoid risk. Professor Han presented people with one of two options:

- o A = guarantees a gain of $24,000
- o B = offers a 25% chance of gaining $100,000 and a 75% chance of no gain.

In this situation, most people will choose option A in order to avoid a risk of no gain—this is *risk aversion*. On the other hand, when the choice is …

- o C = a certain loss of $24,000
- o D = a 25% chance of no loss and a 75% chance of losing $100,000

investors overwhelmingly choose to risk the loss of $100,000. This is called *loss aversion*.

Han theorizes that while people are risk-averse regarding gains, they tend to seek risks regarding potential losses because they hate losses far more than they appreciate gains.

Prospect theory is often applied to the choice of an investment portfolio. But unlike traditional finance theory, prospect theory implies that rather than choosing well-diversified portfolios, investors will often do just the opposite.

Han gave an example of his own portfolio, observing that he usually predicts things correctly in his research but finds it much harder to adhere to that when he is trading. He wrote that he was at the time holding two loser stocks because he did not want to realize the loss by selling them. He often goes so far as to sell his profitable stocks just to funnel more money into the losing ones, convinced that they will rebound and he will regain his money more quickly. These same traps keep investors from holding a diversified portfolio because they focus all of their energy on a handful of individual investments.

Since stock prices see daily variations, the more frequently an investor evaluates his portfolio, the more likely it is that he will suffer from loss aversion. However, this is not an issue for the investor who lets things ride for months or a year, during which time fluctuations even out. For the most part, the latter investor will have a lower perception of stock market risk.

This chapter has been dedicated to the issue of money, and this book is about the workings of the marketplace. It is, therefore, fitting to end this chapter on the subject of *business intelligence.*

Business Intelligence

The term 'business intelligence' is defined by Webopedia as "tools, systems, and strategies that create analysis and planning processes within a corporation. The field of business intelligence optimizes business decisions and drives success through the combination of technology, business processes, and data." This is not the meaning I give to this term in this section. Rather, I denote 'business intelligence' as that which considers what special talents, skill sets, experience, and wisdom allow some people to succeed while others fail or merely operate in a mediocre company.

Does success in the marketplace depend on some unique emotional intelligence, special talent, deep pockets, leadership qualities, or business acumen? In its most basic sense, Merriam-Webster dictionary refers to 'intelligence' as "the ability to learn or understand or to deal with new or trying situations and the skilled use of reason." In the same way, 'business intelligence' is described by business thought leaders as "the essential capacity for success in the marketplace: being able to handle the challenges and crises of the day adeptly; to apply expertise in discovering solutions as needed, and to do all that in ways that add value."

What might the key abilities of 'business intelligence' include? The data trail leads us to the research of Harvard Professor David McClelland, who summed up those unique abilities and talents as falling into three basic domains: "cognitive astuteness, or the ability to learn and to think strategically; technical expertise, or the essential crafts involved in getting the work done, and emotional intelligence, the ability to manage ourselves and our relationships."[19]

A further question to be asked is whether a good knowledge of economics, mathematics, business administration, and the science of decision-making can promote business success. Renowned authors Lennick and Kiel answer this question in the affirmative, offering that emotional intelligence is now commonly regarded as critical to success in the marketplace. However, they point out that their research has brought them to the conclusion that emotional intelligence was insufficient to "assure consistent, long-term performance."[20]

Given that emotional intelligence alone will not ensure the longevity of a successful corporation, something else is needed, which Lennick and Kriel ascribe to 'moral intelligence' as being "at the heart of long-lasting business success."[21] In discussing 'moral intelligence,' they include behavior traits, saying, "leaders and their organizations acted in concert with certain core universal principles, including integrity, responsibility, compassion, and forgiveness."[22] Leaders must not only behave morally but also make financially smart decisions.

The Ethics Resource Center in Washington, D.C., agrees with the importance of ethical behavior in organizational success and states that "companies that are dedicated to doing the right thing, have a written commitment to social responsibility, and act on it consistently are more profitable than those who don't."[23] James Burke, Chairman of Johnson and Johnson at the time, agrees: "If you invested $30,000 in a composite of the Dow Jones thirty years ago, it would be worth $134,000 today. If you had put that $30,000 into these [socially and ethically responsible] firms - $2,000 into each of the fifteen [in the study] - it would now be worth over $1 million."[24]

It seems evident that business intelligence is only intelligence if it leads to a sustainable, long-term, profitable business. To be sustainable and provide long-term performance that is profitable, both emotional and moral intelligence are key ingredients. Another essential criterion is managing partnerships, a trait well known in the business of family.

Business Relationships

Researchers at Booz Allen Hamilton and Northwestern University's Kellogg School of Management found in a study of Fortune 1,000 companies that the most financially successful companies are more focused on relationships than sales. People do not like to be sold; they like to be heard and their needs addressed. The study also revealed that these companies and their sales teams deploy a consistent process to build relationships, which is their success differentiator.[25]

Building good business relationships requires, amongst others, time, effort, transparency, integrity, honesty, respect, and patience. Each relationship will have its unique differences, but one denominator will always pay good dividends – your client's best interests must always be foremost in your mind. Winning the heart of the client can only be done with honest and sincere effort. Respect is at the heart of building business relationships. It is the glue that holds together the functioning of teams, partnerships, and managing relationships.

If your relational approach is not heartfelt, it won't work. Relationships are quickly broken through a phony attitude or false façade. Successful companies are service-oriented and filled with people who want to help others get quality and value for their money.

In essence, another way to describe the marketplace is the 'people industry.' Those who are successful in this industry are those who focus on building good and long-lasting relationships. It is not within the scope of this manuscript to delve into the mechanics of fostering good relationships; but needful to raise a big red flag that misplacing your trust and confidence in the wrong partners can potentially be fatal to your organization. Always bear in mind that, at times, your understanding of 'partnership' may be very different from that of some of your business partners.

Outsmart

My father often said to me: *"Get smart. Outsmart."* And those words have stayed with me through every financial challenge, every coded system, and every boardroom negotiation. When it comes to the hidden mechanics of the marketplace - the codes that shape choices, trap intentions, and manipulate outcomes - success does not come from flattery, charisma, or quick decisions. It comes from wisdom. And from faith.

Understanding basic economic and mathematical principles is useful. But more powerful still is the awareness that many who craft these codes from positions of influence forget one timeless truth: *they, too, will one day be held accountable.*

One of the most important distinctions I've offered in this chapter is how we define economics. While many see it as the study of money, I believe economics is fundamentally about human behavior. If we embrace that perspective, it inevitably leads us beyond numbers and charts into the inner world of motives, patterns, and decisions. It leads us to the next layers of decoding from the chapters that follow.

To close, I leave you with the image of a man who once went to request an overdraft at the bank. When the manager invited him to "take a seat," the man humbly replied, *"I'm quite comfortable on my knees, thank you."*

There's wisdom in that posture - a reminder that humility and prayer are more powerful than profit and prestige. May we carry that same posture forward as we prepare to explore the next chapters behind the codes.

CHAPTER 3
THE CODED LANGUAGE

"Then the king instructed Ashpenaz, the master of his
eunuchs, to bring some of the children of Israel and some of
the king's descendants and some of the nobles.... whom they
might teach the language and literature of the Chaldeans."

(Daniel 1:3-4)

The Chaldean Language

In the opening chapter of the Book of Daniel, we encounter a
profound moment: King Nebuchadnezzar of Babylon commands
his chief official to bring young men of nobility and wisdom from
Jerusalem - those possessing knowledge, insight, and quick
understanding - to be taught the language and literature of the
Chaldeans. This was not a superficial educational gesture; it was a

strategic move to immerse future leaders in the codes and systems that governed Babylonian power structures. In modern terms, this was the equivalent of learning to decode the marketplace - understanding its hidden language, values, and operational frameworks. Even as far back as the 6th century BC, there was an acute awareness that influence was tied not just to military might or political conquest but to mastery of knowledge systems.

What's striking is that this scene doesn't open with grand images of palace construction or declarations of dominion. Instead, it gives primacy to the transmission of knowledge, in its essence, a type of decoding. Nebuchadnezzar's priority was not building more physical kingdoms but embedding ideological ones by teaching the literature of the Chaldeans. In our present age, literature has evolved into financial systems, legal codes, marketing tactics, and behavioral economics. The principle remains the same: to thrive, or even survive, in the marketplace, one must first understand the language it speaks.

In my conversations with both emerging professionals and seasoned business veterans, I hear the same concerns repeated in different tones. The young often ask how to navigate the complex array of opportunities they sense all around them. The more experienced often voice something deeper - a sense of disillusionment or exhaustion. Their questions aren't just about growth anymore; they are pleas for meaning, for freedom from entanglement, for clarity. Whether hopeful or weary, the core issue is often the same: a lack of fluency in the marketplace's hidden codes. As I often remind them, decoding those systems - like Daniel once did - can be the first step toward discernment, liberation, and covenantal alignment.

Just as travelers in a foreign land carry a phrasebook to bridge gaps in understanding, those stepping into the modern marketplace need a decoder - something that reveals not only how the system operates but why. Without it, many move forward with effort but little direction, immersed in a game with rules they barely comprehend. It's not just about doing business more effectively. It's about seeing the marketplace clearly, through a spiritual lens, and choosing to walk a path aligned with a higher purpose, not just economic reward.

Coded Marketplace Language

Let me first say what it is not. It's not the continual statement of one's honesty and integrity. The marketplace will not believe what you say about yourself. They will judge your actions for themselves and formulate their own opinion. Even if you do display clear acts of honesty and integrity, it is my experience that the marketplace is not the forum for you to get an opinion on your character; you need to get that opinion only from those who have your best interests at heart.

This is probably one of the best pieces of advice I can offer, as invariably, you will one day find yourself unjustly criticized in the marketplace as a piece of dirt with no integrity. If these words are familiar, do not fret, you are in good company. If these words are not familiar, I will be keeping a reserved seat just for you.

Mistakes commonly made in the marketplace:

o **Avoid boastful talk about yourself.**

Sadly, people, in general, love to talk about themselves. If you boast about yourself or talk too much, you will lose contracts because the market makers are generally not interested in others, merely in their own success.

So, how do you go about winning contracts in the marketplace? First, if you want to gain clients, demonstrate that you care by giving the client space to speak. Dale Carnegie summed it up well when he said, "You can make more friends in two months by becoming interested in other people than you can in two years by trying to get other people interested in you."[26]

Market makers are mostly (well, at least 90% of the time) interested in themselves, so make every effort to forget about yourself and focus on the person you are dealing with and their needs.

This leads to the second way in which to secure contracts: by understanding client expectations and then outperforming those expectations. In today's marketplace, customers are demanding more than ever, expecting to get what they want when they want it, and often requiring it to be customized to suit their needs. If they do not get what they seek from one company, they can easily obtain it from another. By listening carefully and then outperforming customer expectations, you are in a better position to create what Ken Blanchard called 'Raving Fans.'[27]

How do you turn clients into 'Raving Fans'? By achieving the level of service excellence that turns them into an advocate of your products or services in the marketplace. Recognize that competitors can derail your business ambitions and choose to compete rather than serve you with their self-interests.

o **Don't get hastily into the boxing ring.**

Would you readily have entered the boxing ring to face Muhammad Ali? If you even contemplate that for a moment, you will quickly realize that he was superbly conditioned, both physically and mentally, for the rigors of boxing, while you are not! Countless rounds of combat served to toughen his resolve and provide him with hard-earned experience.

In the same way, do not act too hastily and accept a fight with a skilled combatant. Like these great heavyweight champions, the combatant has encountered numerous troubles in their career, so he/she is fit for the commercial boxing ring! You are probably not at their level of discipline, resolve, and experience, and are setting yourself up for a financial and emotional knockout blow. Avoid the ring if you can; it only leads to pain and injury.

o **Understand the prejudice directed at 'Christian' talk.**

The 'C' word makes the marketplace flinch, which is often perceived with unfashionable connotations of a glassy-eyed zealot. Combatants have no knee-jerk reaction to 'Anglican' or 'Methodist,' but they do react to the term 'Christian.' This is so because the word 'Christian' to the combatant smacks not of religion but religiosity, which is off-putting to them, being concerned that Christians will continually evangelize. Combatants have a deep-seated perception that Christians will prophesy to them that the devil will continually haunt those who do not turn to Jesus.

Our companies, like many other businesses, during the early 2000s, chose to publish a statement of values. The reasoning at the time was that in the absence of stating your own values, the marketplace forms its own opinion of what is inherently of value to your business. In addition, clients who associate with your values or guiding principles develop a deeper association with the business and its product and continue to do business with you. After a serious evaluation, our executive team settled on the following set of values: Christ-centered, family-focused, relationship-minded, and profitable with excellence.

After publishing these values on our website, in our corporate literature, and on certain elements of the corporate correspondence, we continued our normal course of business with these values set as the standard against which our conduct was measured. Never once did anyone challenge the last three on the list; however, we were constantly challenged and even attacked because we had chosen to state 'Christ-centered.' I initially naïvely thought that we had transgressed the basic rule of never discussing politics, religion, or sex, but in time, I came to realize that the deep-seated perception of 'Christians' held by competitors or even the general public was manifesting itself.

I well understand this deep-seated prejudice, but my team and I will resolutely stand and talk about Christian values, just ducking better when the rocks start flying in our direction. Herein we are guided by the wise words of Charles Spurgeon: "Etiquette, nowadays, often demands of a Christian that he should not intrude his religion upon company. Out on such etiquette! It is the etiquette of hell. True courtesy to my fellow's soul makes me speak to him, if I believe that soul to be in danger."

o **Understand that it is foolish to shake hands on a deal.**

Deal makers use handshakes as flattery to undermine your resolve and manipulate you into believing there may be true friendship, faith, and trust in the relationship. The subject of the 'handshake' is so important that I have dealt with it in much more detail below (I think you are going to enjoy this observation).

The Handshake

When it comes to conveying goodwill and instilling confidence, a team of researchers found that nothing beats an old-fashioned handshake. The researchers say the gesture can reinforce positive impressions and even undo bad ones.

The claim comes from a team at the University of Illinois in the US, who had brain scans done on eighteen people while they watched footage of businessmen meeting for the first time.[28] Important areas of the brain responded to witnessing the handshakes, and Dr. Sandra Dolcos stated that the results showed the gesture had 'a positive impact.'

In addition, the *nucleus accumbens* – a region of the brain that is sensitive to rewards – showed greater activity while watching meetings that included handshakes than those without, demonstrating "the positive effect of a handshake on social evaluation." The psychologist added, "It not only increases the positive effect toward a favorable interaction, but it also diminishes the impact of a negative impression."

Dr. Douglas Fields, a neurobiologist and author, agrees with the importance of the handshake and states that a fleeting gripping of palms accompanied by little or no verbal exchange of substance is priceless. "That's because handshaking and body language, in general, communicate powerfully and deeply about the internal state and intentions of other people," he states.[29]

The positive effect of the handshake on social evaluation can, however, return to sting you, as famously discovered by Microsoft founder Bill Gates when shaking hands with South Korean President Park Geun-hye in April 2013. Mr. Gates casually used one hand to greet the President with the other tucked in the pocket of his trousers, only to be slammed by the Korean media for doing so, as it appeared to be a dismissive and rude gesture, even though Mr. Gates did this in innocence.

I don't think any reader would disagree with the finding that handshakes enhance one's social image. Richard 'The Old Man' Harrison, in the popular TV reality series based on the famous Las Vegas pawn broker shop, shows how the old style 'handshake' is correctly applied and says that "handshaking is a universal type of communication which communicates 'deal done' at the end of every agreement." He goes on to say that "when you cut a deal, it is customary to handshake." He, however, slips in something interesting in an interview on the handshake when he said, "Back in the Roman days, the handshake was used more as a 'signal of power' than now."

Merchants understand this hidden language and 'signal of power' very well and use it as a manipulative tool to disarm you. There are many good lessons to be learnt from the handshake, but I do not embrace it because my brutal experience has shown me that in the majority of the cases I have observed, Merchants contort the handshake, changing its original, innocent gesture into a negative one, to gain competitive advantage and make you feel guilty that you somehow have not lived up to your end of the bargain.

For a better understanding of the handshake, one needs to appreciate the history of its origin. The first known depiction of a handshake was found in Egyptian frescoes dating back to around 2,800 BC. The handshake was symbolic of a suspension of danger and always featured the right hand (because it was the weapon-wielding hand), showing that the greeter's weapon hand was unarmed.[30]

In Roman times, the handshake was an arm clasp, with each man clasping just below the elbow of the other. This gesture provided a better opportunity to feel for daggers hidden in sleeves. Medieval knights took further precautions by adding a shake to the clasp to dislodge any hidden weapons, and thus the handshake was born.[31]

I agree with the positive effect of a handshake on social evaluation, but I strongly urge people in the marketplace to use the goodwill gesture with maximum caution and clasp their hand just below the elbow of the Merchant to provide you with the best opportunity to "feel for daggers hidden in sleeves."

The Perfect Handshake Equation

To seal more car deals, Chevrolet UK looked to arm its sales force with the perfect weapon of confidence: an unstoppable handshake. The challenge, intended only to be humorous for marketing purposes, set off the imagination of writer Professor Geoffrey Beattie, former Head of Psychological Sciences at the University of Manchester. After much reflection, Professor Beattie created an equation based on what he called PH – the Perfect Handshake.[32]

$$PH = \sqrt{(e^2 + ve^2)(d^2) + (cg + dr)^2 + \pi\{(4< s >^2)(4^2)\}^2 + (vi + t + te)^2 + \{(4^2)(4^2)\}^2}$$

I find it mind-boggling that an apparently simple concept, such as a handshake, can be analyzed so deeply, albeit as a marketing gimmick. Naturally, the variables are too numerous and complicated to list here (there are about sixty or so), including an exhaustive list of factors such as eye contact, completeness of grip, as well as dryness and temperature of hands.

Readers are not expected to work it out or understand it, but apart from the touch of fun, it serves to demonstrate that there is far more to a handshake than most people think. Invariably, you will shake hands at some time, but clarify that your goal is to reach an agreement that is mutually acceptable.

The Handshake Daggers

There's a reason the "handcuff and dagger" tattoo remains a popular symbol - it reflects a hard truth. Contracts, with all their length and legalese, often feel restrictive and intimidating. People tend to avoid them, not because they don't recognize their value, but because they feel bound by them - handcuffed to terms they barely understand.

Yet, the alternative - relying on a handshake - offers only the illusion of freedom. While a handshake might feel more human and more trusting, it leaves too much to memory, interpretation, and unspoken expectations. Even two sincere individuals can walk away from the same conversation with entirely different understandings. And when the agreement breaks down, it's rarely the naïve party that prevails. That's why experienced Merchants prefer handshake deals - because they've mastered how to bend them to their advantage. As the saying goes, "The Merchant's tweety bird always wins."

In marketplace culture, this inform approach is not casual - it's calculated. The handshake becomes a tool of psychological control, cloaked in civility. Whether it's a lack of documentation or the false comfort of verbal assurance, these agreements often lead to misunderstanding, imbalance, and regret. The spiritual takeaway is clear: deception often masquerades as trust. When we operate in the marketplace without clarity and covenant, we risk becoming complicit in systems that value manipulation over truth.

Before entering any agreement, ask yourself - are you engaging from a position of discernment or just hoping for fairness? One path leads to covenantal wisdom. The other to confusion, resentment, and bondage. Consider these pointers:

o   The Merchant is often a master at the sales pitch, very capable of making you feel that the deal in front of you is an incredible opportunity. Facing the prospect of such a great windfall, you may feel that you do not want the other party to think the deal through too much. They may discover that it favors you too much. Guess what? The Merchant is thinking the same thing about you. He may have set you up and does not want you to lift the curtain to the reality of what you have bought into.

o   The Merchant may maneuver you to trust him or her with a handshake. If the Merchant is trustworthy, still follow the old Richard Nixon (37th US President) line, "Trust everyone, but cut the cards." Within a card game, the dealer generally shuffles the cards. The cards are then passed along to an opposing player to cut the cards, meaning to lift up part of the cards and place it under the remaining part of the deck. This means that, should the dealer have managed to stack the deck in his favor, such cheating is negated. This phrase is, in effect, saying – trust everyone but put safeguards in place just in case everyone cannot be trusted.

o   You may feel the deal is far too complicated to record in writing. Odds are that it's not too complicated to put into writing, but you simply don't completely understand it just yet. Take the time to write out the deal and clear up any points you don't understand with the other party as you go along. You need to ensure that you are fully aware of the whole picture and its implications. If you can't understand the full picture as a party to the agreement, how will a judge or jury understand the agreement when you try to enforce it?

o Where has the other person's hand been? A danger of the handshake agreement, which we may not consider in the excitement of sealing the deal, is that we have no record of what other agreements our 'partner' has made in a similar way. Whose hands have the merchants been shaking prior to our agreement? How can we review the Merchant's track record in keeping their end of the bargain if we cannot easily discover what bargains they have made? Ask yourself the question: *How do I know that the hand I am shaking is clean and virus-free?*

o Finally, while the Merchant is shaking with one hand, the other hand may be behind their back, forefinger and middle finger crossed because everyone knows that this gesture soothes the conscience and nullifies anything or everything you've agreed to do.

We should be cautious that the Merchant and his accomplices may come along with a workshop full of willing hands and tools that may shake for any price. If you find yourself in a situation where you are about to make a deal based on only a handshake, stop and ensure that you are not exposing your vulnerability or selling yourself short.

Key Phrases in the Marketplace Handbook

John was invited by his friend to attend the Joke Telling Society's annual dinner. After a delicious meal, one gentleman went up to the microphone and said, "226." Everyone began laughing. The next person walked to the microphone and said, "73," and again, there was laughter all around. Obviously, this seemed strange, and so John asked his friend for an explanation.

"Oh," he said, "we have so many jokes that they are all numbered in a handbook, and everyone here knows the numbering. To save time, you call out the number, and people appreciate the joke."

That made sense, and so John asked if he could have a turn. He made his way to the microphone and announced, "314."

No one laughed. "What's wrong?" he asked his friend. "Well, it's the way you tell it!" came the reply.

When you have been active in the marketplace for over ten decades, as our family businesses have, you start recognizing these numbers or codes; it's unspoken, but the skilled know exactly what's being said:

o **Know the bottom line?** No need for lofty promises, cleverly worded marketing plans, or lots of fanfare. In the marketplace, the buyer wants to know how much it will cost, when they can expect to receive it, and how much money they will make in return for their efforts.

A true story is told of how a multinational first won a big government courier contract. There were many tenders and many sessions of boardroom discussions. Everyone who tendered had spent considerable sums to market and sell their product to the appropriate government agencies, except for one mad-looking Einstein lookalike. He arrived at the meeting scruffily dressed and with only a poster under his arm. When he unrolled the poster for the formal-looking officials, it only had a picture of a Coke bottle. The Einstein lookalike glibly said, "Hey guys, we are in more countries than Coke." Einstein's courier company duly won the contract!

o **Be as wise as a serpent and as gentle as a dove**.[33] People who thrive in the marketplace are shrewd. A shrewd person is both wise and insightful. They can interpret nuances and inferences in both written and spoken text, they can 'pick up on the subtext,' and they possess extensive real-world street smarts. Shrewd people know that the order in which events occur is crucial to the success of a deal. They know when to withdraw and when to act, and they know what to say and what not to reveal.

An imaginary tale is shared about two friends. Joe is very bright and analytical, while Sam is a true entrepreneur. While drinking beer at the local pub with their dogs, Sam (with his Chihuahua at his side) says to Joe (with his Doberman) that he wants to go and eat at the fancy restaurant across the street. Joe replies that the doorman will not allow their dogs into the

64

restaurant, but Sam counter-replies that they must simply make an entrepreneurial plan and pretend they are blind and that these are guide dogs. Joe agrees with the plan and says he will go first.

Lo and behold, the doorman stops Joe and says, "Sorry, Sir, we do not allow dogs in our restaurant," and Joe immediately counters, "This is my guide dog." The confused doorman questions Joe. "Sir, do they now use Dobermans as guide dogs?" to which Joe replies, "Of course."

Sam observes Joe's success, and after a few minutes, he approaches the doorman with his Chihuahua. The doorman looks on in confusion because just a few moments ago, he let who he thought was the same person into the restaurant with a Doberman, and now here he is again with a Chihuahua. He questions Sam, "But Sir, surely you cannot say they also use Chihuahuas as guide dogs?" to which the shrewd and insightful Sam replies, "What?? Do you want to tell me they gave me a Chihuahua?"

Now, many people can claim to be shrewd because they possess the abilities or qualities demonstrated by Sam. However, few have the innate ability to operate with the gentleness of a dove. This rare breed of entrepreneur never exploits naïve people or an innocent situation for their own gain. This unusual merchant considers the impact on both society and the environment before making their decision, and this truly remarkable individual chooses to create a more harmonious win-win environment rather than a winner-take-all context. By being 'gentle as a dove', they are not presenting themselves as weak and defenseless but rather shrewdly implementing the preferential deal for all parties using the insight they have in both the present and future context.

o   **Work hard**. The marketplace watches your work ethic. You need to set an example by working hard. I remember once advertising for a senior secretarial position, and a devout Christian lady applied. When she was asked why she wanted the job, she replied that working for this family would help her do more Bible study during working hours! Don't start to define your work as "sightseeing and eating with a dull session in the middle."

o   **Build your network**. It's not what you know but who you know – and how well you treat them! Your network will be established only on the back of your continually delivering on your promises.

My brother Brian is a good sales agent and happens to be an expert in food and wine, known by his friends and family as a great entertainer. Brian has a firm policy that if you want to 'clinch a deal,' you need to go the 'extra mile.' Brian goes the extra mile by employing his natural talent for hospitality and using his knowledge of food and wine to his advantage.

Brian's company hospitality bill is always very high, adding to the frustration of the administration staff who have to reconcile his entertainment expenses against his commission payments.

Fortunately, his earnings and value to the company are evident that he has gone the 'extra mile' to earn great rewards.

Many a deal Brian has concluded after having entertained the prospective purchaser. Brian attributes his success to his policy that he treats every prospect like he would a 'celebrity' because people want to be important and enjoy being made to feel special. What Brian was doing was increasing his circle of influence. The prospect, in many instances, became the client of Brian and, due to the enjoyable experience of Brian's hospitality, often reciprocated his generosity by inviting him to their table, where other prospective buyers and sellers probably sat. So the circle of influence increased, and referral business was the primary source that generated income for Brian and, in the end, our Company.

o   **Be careful before borrowing.** A wise individual once said: "Before you borrow, ask yourself if the debt will grow you or weigh you?"

Debt should be used strategically to invest in your personal or business growth. Taking on a mortgage, provided that the mortgage repayments are affordable, can be a wise financial decision. However, going into debt for excessive office furnishings just to impress competitors is more likely to stunt the progress of your business rather than support it.

Interestingly, Romans 13:8 encourages us to aim to be debt free, except for the debt of love, which we should never cease to owe or fulfil.

o   **Be aware that there is no such thing as a free lunch**. Every time you receive what appears to be a kind gesture, the person who offered it to you is making a mental note that 'you owe them one.' Be cautious with whom you associate and from whom you receive money or favors.

A company CEO liked a brochure he saw and wanted his in-house marketing team to use a similar format to advertise his hotels. After the first version and quote were presented to print at $20 per unit, the CEO dismissed it and instructed a reduced unit cost price. The cost was then reduced, but so was the brochure's quality. The CEO remained determined by his instruction to obtain a similar effect at a cost of $12 per unit. A month later, the in-house marketing team had still not come up with a proposal, and they were rudely summoned by the CEO to get their act together. Shortly after, they came back with a revised one-page brochure with one simple sentence. It read, "There is NO Free Lunch." Obviously, the CEO wanted quality but didn't want to pay for it.

Meanwhile, in the Kruger National Park in South Africa, signs warn: "Do not feed the animals." Park authorities are concerned that the animals will grow dependent and not learn to take care of themselves.

o **Be assured that what goes around comes around**. The marketplace is small. What you sow, you will most definitely reap! This applies both in a positive and negative context. As a positive example, our business established an educational program that had its focus on entrepreneurship and business leadership. What made the program unique was that it was wholly sponsored.

Offering this program, for no other reason than Corporate Social Responsibility, we found that many of the learners, already university graduates and successful professionals, were keen to work in our organization. The program proved to be our most consistent and reliable recruitment mechanism, and we welcomed many talented individuals to our business through it.

o **Clearly define your needs**. If you do not clearly describe your requirements, you may find yourself in the undesirable position that my grandfather found himself in when he ordered four tons of rice, and 400 tons of rice was delivered because the number four was probably not written down in words.

On another occasion, our company once advertised in the local news for a travel agent to assist in our travel agency business. The church that I was attending at the time spotted the advertisement and graciously offered to announce in their church bulletin that we were offering employment to an appropriate agent, although they neglected to mention that it was for a travel agency business. One of the church members applied, but he was an electrician. When we interviewed him, we asked him how much travel experience he had, to which he duly replied, "I travel long distances every day to meet the needs of my clients. You can never tell in which home there will be an electrical fault."

Avoid acting like the Managing Director who sent an urgent memo to his senior staff: "We must avoid all unnecessary duplication of communication. I cannot repeat this too many times."

o **Include these criteria: People, planet, profit.** First coined in 1994 by John Elkington, the founder of a British consultancy called SustainAbility, the notion of businesses measuring their contribution against a 'triple bottom line' is proposed.

The triple bottom line includes people, the planet, and profit. 'People' represents fair and beneficial business practices toward both the workforce and the community in which a company conducts its business. 'Planet' refers to sustainable environmental practices, and 'Profit' is the economic value created by the company after deducting the cost of all inputs, including the cost of the capital tied up. This 'triple bottom line' concept is asking companies to achieve their financial results in collaboration with their available resources and not at their expense of them. Sustainability, multi-generational thinking, and contribution are all biblical principles, and Proverbs 13:22 instructs, "A good man leaves an inheritance to his children's children, but the wealth of the sinner is stored up for the righteous."

o   **Never close a sale.** I have met several successful salespeople over the years and often engaged with them in my effort to unlock the secret to sales. Sales are crucial for any business, and so pursuing these secrets is a clear pursuit for any entrepreneur. Each one of these sales professionals offered a similar response, perhaps phrased in a different way.

Never 'close' a sale as it implies an end and that the seller has extracted what they want from the buyer. Rather 'open' mutually beneficial relationships by constantly offering the client what they need to enhance their business or personal life. Many of the top sales professionals would rather walk away from a lucrative, once-off, relationship-ending commission because the prudent individual knows that you can shear a sheep every season, but you can only skin it once.

o   **Be remarkable.** Seth Godin's book entitled *Purple Cow*[34] provides a lovely illustration of the concept of being remarkable. He asks if the reader has ever noticed the faces of children in a car when they pass a field filled with brown cows. Some big, some small, but all of them brown. He notes that for the first few minutes, it shrieks with excitement, but then it's back to silence. Why? The answer is simple: *after you have seen one field of brown cows, they become boring!* Brown cows, like many companies, are boring! What's required is a purple cow amongst the brown cows - a cow that stands out. Now, that would be remarkable.

Many of the companies we read about today are like brown cows: functional but boring. Businesses should aim to be a purple cow amongst the rest of the herd and be remarkable. They should be the first to market innovative products in their chosen sectors. They should want to provide clients with access to benefits and value they cannot access themselves, and they should enable clients, through their service, to remark positively about the experience they have doing business together.

o **Respect the 'Alpha-dog' principle.** In each animal group – pack, troop, or pride – there is a dominant leader, the Alpha male. When you're in the Alpha male's territory, you abide by their rules and operate within their prescribed ways. Any young upstart or older competitor is quickly confronted and put in their place.

If you are observant, you will notice that the office reception, board room, or meeting room of corporations most often have the hand of that business' 'Alpha-dog' in the décor, setting, environment, and mood. When you are in their territory, respect it and their ways. Let the Alpha establish the meeting's tone and decide on the subsequent action steps. Find your place within the group and subtly contribute to the conversation. Don't try to upstage or outperform them in their own territory, or you might well encounter the territorial aggression of the Alpha dog.

o **Remain receptive**. In the textbooks on business management, there is often a serious focus on developing a strategy and executing a detailed plan to achieve that strategy. Of course, there

72

is nothing wrong with that, but my experience is that as an entrepreneur, strategy is often amended or even put aside when presented with an opportunity. You will only notice or entertain an opportunity if you 'remain receptive' or open to the thought of new things. Sometimes, your carefully constructed plans pan out, and sometimes, you stumble into a life-altering opportunity.

I'm reminded of John Wood, a senior executive with Microsoft, who, during a three-month sabbatical, chose to hike in Nepal. When he noticed that the rural schools had no books in their libraries, he was 'receptive' to a new opportunity. On leaving Microsoft in 2000, he established 'Room to Read,' which donates books to rural communities. Today, they are a global organization dedicated to promoting and enabling education through programs focused on literacy and gender equality in education. They build schools, create a library, and publish children's books in the local language. They currently work in several countries where the programs have benefited more than eight million children.[35]

o   **Stand firm until 'The 11th Hour.'** A business associate once told me during a breakfast session that he was due to pay his bankers a large sum of money within hours, as it related to interest on a property mortgage. I asked if he was able to do so, and he shared that after serious discussions with several investors, he had been able to raise the funds required just prior to our meeting!

In business, you need to have nerves of steel and be willing to hold your position without flinching in the face of serious deadlines. Usually, the solution or strategy only manifests itself close to the deadline, or what is called 'The 11th Hour.'

We would all like to operate in a business world where everyone plays by the rules, everything runs according to schedule, and debtors are paid on time, but the reality is quite different. Using all the time at your disposal and being able to 'hang tough' when things are not easy is what separates the best from the good.

o **Be cautious of a reconciled enemy.** It is dangerous to place too quickly confidence in a reconciled enemy because even if there has been a level of reconciliation, it takes time and testing before you can be sure that the relationship is sincere. There is a real danger that the 'change of heart' is based on pragmatic or political motives, in which case it will only take a change of circumstance or a climate where there is an opportunity to strike again with minimal consequence for their posture to be reversed.

There is an interesting biblical parallel to illustrate this, which is found in the story of King David. The initial period of David's reign was exemplary, and his kingdom was rapidly expanding as he succeeded in combining both Israel and Judah into a united kingdom, driving out Israel's enemies. However, David made a disastrous mistake when he chose to remain in Jerusalem while his generals, advisors, and armies were away fighting a war. One fateful night, he saw Bathsheba bathing on a rooftop, summoned her, seduced her, and impregnated her, then compounded his error by arranging for the death of her husband, Uriah.

What is less known is that Bathsheba was the daughter of Eliam, one of David's thirty mighty men, who was himself the son of Ahithophel, one of David's chief advisors from David's own tribe. Bathsheba was, therefore, the granddaughter of one of David's closest advisors. The scandal remained secret for a while until David was exposed by Nathan, the prophet, who not only pronounced that the child that had been conceived would die but that there would be trouble and violence within David's own house.

The details of what happened next are not recorded for us, but it does not take much imagination to realize that these events had major interpersonal ramifications. In a patriarchal age, the honor of Ahithophel's family was severely compromised by what had occurred. David did subsequently do the 'right thing' by taking Bathsheba to be his wife, but the relational damage had already been done. No doubt because David was King, Ahithophel had to carry on, but the offence clearly festered because a few years later, David's son Absalom led a rebellion against his father, and Ahithophel quickly joined Absalom's side and used his talents and knowledge to aid the rebellion. If his advice had been followed, it would almost certainly have led to David's destruction; it was only divine intervention that caused it to be ignored.

I have seen this pattern outwork my times; those who you thought were for you turn out to be against you because they wait for the opportunity to take revenge on a festering offence.

o **Surround yourself with the right people.** The business world is rewarding but brings with it challenges, pressure, and sleep deprivation. Don't compound the situation by having eternally negative, emotionally draining, or unreasonably demanding people within your immediate team. Yes, we all need a good dose of reality at times and the varied input from a diverse team, but that can be achieved through the input of realist, skilled, and well-meaning people, and by this, I certainly do not refer to just 'yes, men.' Take the time to carefully appoint those who operate alongside you and seek people who can add relevant professional value while making the journey light.

Lastly, the marketplace is a strange place, and sometimes, there is much truth to the humorous anecdotes about the bazaar. One such truth is succinctly described by Harry Chapman, Financial Director of Think, when setting Committee Rules:[36]

1. Never arrive on time, or you will be stamped a beginner.

2. Don't say anything until the meeting is half over; this stamps you as being wise.

3. Be as vague as possible; this prevents irritating others.

4. When in doubt, suggest that a subcommittee be appointed.

5. Be the first to move for adjournment; this will make you popular – it's what everyone is waiting for.

Foolishness versus Wisdom

As the marketplace language is infected with foolish jargon, we need to lastly consider the ways of a fool versus those of the wise. What is it that keeps a fool from being wise? Scripture gives us the answer: "The way of a fool is right in his own eyes,"[37] whereas the astute is not wise in his own eyes.[38]

A fool is simply a person who acts unwisely or imprudently. Although a wise individual acts directly contrary to that of a fool, his/her distinguishing feature is their fear of God, which, according to the wise King Solomon, is 'man's all.'[39]

A fool will always mistakenly believe he is in the right in everything he does and, therefore, seeks no advice because he does not apprehend that he needs it; he is sure he knows the way and, therefore, never seeks other alternatives. According to the renowned Christian Bible commentator Matthew Henry:

> *"There is not a greater enemy to the power of religion, and the fear of God in the heart, than conceitedness of our own wisdom. Those that have an opinion of their own sufficiency think it below them, and disparagement to them, to take their measures from, much more to hamper themselves with, religion's rules."*

The fool's rule is to be governed by his eyes, not by conscience or accepted norms, and therefore, walks in the way of his heart and experience – his will is always his law.

The wise individual, on the contrary, not only desires to have counsel given to him/her but also hearkens to counsel. The wise are reserved with their own judgment and place value on the direction of those who are wise and good. This is in line with the guidance of Proverbs 1:5: "A wise man will hear and increase learning, and a man of understanding will attain wise counsel."

Being in commercial partnerships or contracts with wise people is indeed a rare thing, as the marketplace is littered with unwise actions. The wise welcome guidance, but tread carefully when directing or instructing a fool; he will hate you for it because a "fool has no delight in understanding, but in expressing his own heart"[40] and "if you speak in the hearing of a fool … he will despise the wisdom of your words."[41]

A gentle reproof will positively enter not only into the head but also into the heart of a wise man. However, like Pharaoh, who remained hard under all the plagues of Egypt, a hundred stripes are not enough for a fool to make him sensible of his errors.[42]

In a culture of honor, we should celebrate who the person is without stumbling over who he/she is not. This is sadly not the thought process of a fool; therefore, "answer not a fool according to his folly, lest you also be like him."[43] When confronted by a fool, and this will be very often in the marketplace, remember that an elephant should not feel threatened by an ant that is spitting at it. However, in a fight with a skunk, you might win the fight, but you will smell awful afterwards.

I experienced first-hand the dangers of debating with fools. Our Company was once in partnership with a group of astute businessmen, and the partnership was highly profitable. My sincere pieces of advice on how to restructure the business were perceived as offensive because our partners were completely certain they needed no guidance from a man younger than themselves. The mistake our partners made was that while they recognized my youth, they failed to understand the depth of my loyalty to them. Although I greatly respected the wisdom of these successful businessmen and gleaned from their experience, they did not glean from my own inherited talent and paid dearly for the error. The once successful partnership was destroyed because of the foolish decisions of our partners, their unwillingness to learn, and their distrust of those who loved them.

Cautious, Prudent, and Measured

A principle to apply in all marketplace dealings is to strive to be as cautious, prudent, and measured as possible. It is, however, essential that we live in a constant state of dependence upon God,[44] as He can do all things which we trust in Him for. Scripture cautions us to take heed of misplacing our confidence - those who trust in God truly will *trust in Him only.*

I have been comforted and protected by my knowledge of the marketplace codes, passed on to me by my grandfather and father. In fact, this knowledge mixed with faith 'saved my bacon' on many occasions. When the lion roars against you, you must choose either fight or flight, confront or run, live or die. Decoding the marketplace will go a long way toward helping you to confront where required and to overcome without falling into the duplicitous hands of those who seek their own gain at your expense.

CHAPTER 4
CODED ARROWS

"No weapon formed against you shall prosper, and every tongue which rises against you [the person] in judgment, You [the Lord] shall condemn."

(Isaiah 54:17)

The Quiet War

The coded arrow - a phrase cloaked in shadow and steel - speaks not of bloodshed, but of silent wars waged in boardrooms and backchannels. They are the quiet, calculated strikes where rivals fall not by blade, but by strategy; not by gun, but through subtlety. In this corporate theatre, the kill is metaphorical, yet the ruin is real, executed through cunning, control, and deep-seated malice.

The dark mindset behind a metaphorical 'coded arrow' often unleashes devastating consequences, inflicting great harm on those caught unwittingly in its path. In many cases, the coded arrow serves as a silenced weapon - its flight hushed, its purpose cloaked - where the instigator weaves subtlety and cunning to veil intent, letting malice move forward in ghostlike silence.

Makers of coded arrows are consumed by the craft of silence, ever striving for sleeker shadows. In their pursuit of modern mastery, they forge and refine new arrows - elegant in form, elusive in flight, and ever more intricate in their quiet intent yet operate with such subtlety as to earn for themselves the name 'silent weapons,' hence my reference to the word 'coded arrows' (because 'code' implies 'secrecy').

Makers of Coded Arrows

Unlike conventional weapons, coded arrows are designed not to destroy bodies but to destabilize lives - quietly, systematically, and most often legally. While traditional weapons fire bullets, the coded arrow fires a *situation* - a planned or staged dispute. These are not sudden bouts of aggression but carefully orchestrated moves launched from behind desks rather than battlefields.

The operator of such a weapon - a skilled antagonist - rarely acts alone. They follow orders handed down through a chain of command, echoing the dynamic between a modern-day marksman and their military general. The entire system is structured, intentional, and highly practiced.

What makes the coded arrow especially dangerous is its invisibility. It makes no audible sound and leaves no immediate trace. Daily life goes on, seemingly untouched. Yet, to the trained eye, the damage is unmistakable - mental exhaustion, financial strain, broken trust, and subtle control. The attack is real, but it is engineered to bypass ordinary perception.

The success of this weapon lies in human psychology. Sudden change sparks resistance. Gradual change? Acceptance. The architects of these arrows understand this deeply, deploying disruption in slow increments that society absorbs without protest. Over time, the psychological pressure builds. People feel it but can't name it. They begin to tolerate dysfunction, unsure whether their discomfort is justified. Most remain silent - afraid of ridicule, isolation, or being labeled paranoid.

And when people don't recognize the attack, they don't seek a defense. The result? A society weakened from within - emotionally, mentally, and spiritually. These arrows, much like weapons of biological warfare, target the very sources of natural and social energy. They dull discernment, drain courage, and cripple mobility. Once weakened, individuals and communities become susceptible to manipulation at every level.

The Spiritually Discerning

The Book of Nehemiah offers a powerful metaphor for the spiritual entrepreneur. As the builders of Jerusalem's wall labored, they held both tools and weapons - one hand on the work, the other on defense. In today's context, the tools might be education, calculators, or digital systems -symbols of construction and progress. The weapons? Cash flow management, discernment, and strategic knowledge - essential defenses against marketplace deception.

Nehemiah and his companions remained in a constant state of readiness, never laying down their weapons, not even when going to fetch water. This posture wasn't just practical; it was prophetic. It reflects the reality of marketplace life: that while we build, we must also guard.

This chapter explores the dual requirement: mastery of business-building techniques and readiness to confront the "coded arrows" that threaten progress. Whatever dysfunctional form these arrows take, success depends on both strategy and spiritual vigilance.

Coded arrows aren't a modern invention. They have ancient origins, hidden in the darker chapters of human history. But today's version is more refined. As an example, it now operates through the overlooked concept of *economic inductance* - a missing link in economic theory that explains how passive, unseen forces accumulate pressure until systems collapse or shift. Understanding this is not just an intellectual exercise; it's the beginning of a spiritual awakening.

Economic Inductance

Those who control the flow of money don't just manage wealth - they shape reality. By steering financial currents, they can quietly rearrange entire economic systems in ways that benefit themselves. This concept lies at the heart of *economic inductance* - the use of power or influence to intentionally induce instability and then profit from the resulting chaos.

Debt, perhaps the most visible coded arrow, serves as a prime example - hence the reason I introduced household debt at the beginning of this book. Wealthy nations extend loans to poorer ones, promising growth and opportunity. In return, these nations surrender valuable assets as collateral. Then, through engineered instability - rising interest rates, inflation, or currency devaluation - the cost of that debt becomes unmanageable. Desperation sets in. To keep up, the borrower must take on even more debt. Eventually, scarcity is manufactured, and pressure is applied. Under the weight of legal obligation and economic chokeholds, the lender seizes the collateral, often natural resources or strategic infrastructure.

These pressures, subtle at first, have real and devastating consequences. Entire countries and corporations crumble under their weight. Wars ignite. Sovereignty collapses. The coded arrow has hit its mark.

But financial manipulation isn't the only modern arrow. Today, technology plays an equally powerful role, controlling not just the movement of currency but also the flow of information across borders. Those who influence the systems behind payment platforms, data infrastructures, and surveillance networks hold a discreet yet formidable power. They decide who can access resources and for what purpose. The world becomes less about ownership and more about permission.

This is the full force of economic inductance: money and information are no longer just tools, but act as weapons. And those who command them hold absolute power. I've seen this power at play time and time again throughout my business life. It seldom announces itself with violence. Instead, it slides beneath the surface, poisoning decisions, dismantling trust, and shaping destinies.

That poison - the coded arrow - doesn't aim for your pocket alone. It aims for your soul. It creates both internal unrest and external hardship. The turmoil it causes isn't random - it's orchestrated. It works by destabilizing your sense of security, your moral compass, your friendships, and your spiritual foundation.

This chapter is included to expose the poisonous coded arrows for what they are and to begin offering countermeasures. While only a few of these arrows can be explored in depth here, understanding them is the first step toward freedom.

False Accusations

In 2002, Brian Banks, at the age of seventeen, was an outstanding U.S. football star at the Polytechnic High School in Long Beach. He had a great future ahead of him and had the potential to go into professional football. During the course of the year, however, he was accused of rape by a classmate, and after a lengthy trial, he was sentenced to five years in prison with an additional five years as a registered sexual offender, during which time he had to wear a tracking device on his ankle.[45] Banks was jailed because he had been given two options: plead guilty to a lesser charge or stand the chance of being jailed for over forty years. As a young man, fearful of jail and unaware of his other options, he took the lesser charge.

He had constantly claimed his innocence. In 2012, Banks was exonerated when the local court overturned the case, freeing this man who had lived with these false accusations and a ruined reputation for ten years. But Brian's dream has come true. In April 2013, he was signed with the Atlanta Falcons and went back into the world of professional football.[46]

A false accusation is a coded arrow with immense venom to destroy the lives of its victim. Such an accusation "refers to a situation where someone claims that another person has committed an illegal or immoral act that they did not actually do."[47] The tongue is an incredibly powerful weapon; it can be used either for poison or medicine. Words used as poison are like the piercings of a sword and cut to the heart. Slanderers, like a sword, wound the reputation of those of whom they are uttered. Secretive talk and evil surmises, like a sword, also divide and cut the bonds of love and friendship.

In a similar way, market manipulators often use elements of truth and exaggeration to sully one's reputation (in one's own eyes as well as those of others). The whole truth is not told. Over the years, thousands of people have found themselves wrongly accused and have had to bear the consequences. In 1 Peter 2:20-23, the innocent are tested, "For what credit is it if, when you are beaten for your faults, you take it patiently? But when you do good and suffer, if you take it patiently, this is commendable before God."

Jesus Christ was innocent of sin but was wrongly accused and crucified as an innocent person. We are called to follow his example because "when He was reviled, did not revile in return; when He suffered, He did not threaten but committed Himself to Him who judges righteously."[48]

The biblical example of Joseph illustrates this principle well. Joseph was wrongly thrown into a pit and sold as a slave by his brothers. Once in Egypt, working for Potiphar, Potiphar's wife wrongly accused him of trying to rape her,[49] and Joseph found himself in prison because of these accusations. Again, Joseph did what was right and soon prospered even within that context, finding himself in the position of second-in-command in the whole of Egypt. God sees when we are falsely accused and will bring about righteousness and justice, but in His own time. Our part is to wait upon the Lord and maintain our trust in Him.

From early boyhood, when I was falsely accused and endured hardship as a result, I did my best to keep possession of my soul, and in that, I found victory. John Milton, the 17th-century English poet and politician, said, "I will not deny but that the best apology against false accusers is silence and sufferance, and honest deeds set against dishonest words."[50] When our reputation is at stake, we would do well not to fight back but immediately bring the false accusations first before God. He alone is the One to whom we should plead our innocence, knowing that a life of integrity would ultimately triumph over every false allegation.

Let the fight in which we engage be restricted solely to a fight of integrity. Vengeance is the Lord's alone.[51] He is the only One who has the wisdom adequate to handle this venomous coded arrow. We are also to respond in a way that is righteous and does not dishonor God or His name.

Betrayal

"Et tu, Brute!" With those immortal words, Julius Caesar, in the great Shakespearean play, breathed his last. He had been betrayed by his friend Decius Brutus. Such betrayal of friendship and partnership not only makes for a good story but also reflects the cold realities of life, where two individuals or companies go their separate ways in a pain-filled moment. Betrayal can be defined as: "To give aid or information to an enemy; to commit treason against; to deliver into the hands of an enemy in violation of a trust or allegiance; to be false or disloyal to; to divulge in a breach of confidence."[52] And, of course, the greatest betrayal of all was suffered by Jesus Christ at the behest of Judas Iscariot.

Betrayal is often a key weapon of deceivers as it may lead one to think that the relationship is a long-standing one, built on trust and a common partnership toward a united end. Instead, betrayal rears its angry head as the realities of the relationship are steadily exposed. As mentioned elsewhere in this book, what looks like a partnership for the mutual benefit of both parties ends in betrayal as the antagonists press into their goals and agenda at the expense of their 'partner.'

These words in a novel about Mary, Queen of Scots, reveal something of the emotion that such betrayal inspires: "Defeat I can endure with cheerfulness, my lady. But betrayal is like taking the wind from my sails or the earth from beneath my feet. It chills my spirits like a rainy day, and all I can do is draw the curtains and cry into my pillow."[53]

Such betrayal occurs in several ways. On a macro level that deals with whole economies, antagonists betray the ordinary individual by setting procedures and processes in place for the management of money, which directly and positively impact governments and organizations at the expense of the average person. Commentator Ivo Mosley, for example, stated, "Our representatives betray us by allowing banks to create the money supply. Money is created in a way that benefits politicians, bankers, and capitalists (entrepreneurs and investors) at the expense of the rest of us. Most of the laws that underpin the process have never even been argued about, let alone voted on, in any legislative assembly. Money creation is managed behind closed doors by those who profit from the process: that is, by politicians, capitalists, and bankers. Knowledge of the laws and procedures is obscure to all but a few."[54]

On a local and regional level, individuals may betray their 'partners' by either deserting them when they find themselves in need or by literally stabbing them in the back to achieve their own ideals. Most of us will encounter both of these coded arrows, and they are certainly very real.

In another sense, individuals have betrayed their customers by focusing on their own needs and requirements at the expense of their clients. Essentially, the focus has become so much on making stakeholders, board members, and shareholders happy that the needs of the individual and client have been relegated to the very bottom of the pile. Skilled archers can betray the trust of those they supposedly serve.

This betrayal is reflected in a variety of ways, one being charging carefully hidden fees so that the company makes more money, which enables it to focus on its corporate clients at the expense of the hundreds and thousands of individuals who have placed their trust in those institutions. More importantly, the betrayal comes in their carefully crafted legal contracts, which are designed to imprison or trap you without your knowledge.

One example of this was when a bank inserted a clause in many of our own property bond contracts, a standard 240-page document, namely that infamous Clause 584 (iii), which I did not see because I fell asleep after page 130. It stated that the company signing this contract is liable for all the other debts owned by my grandmother and grandfather and their blood relations and spouses for the next fifty centuries (this is obviously an exaggeration, but the effect it had on me was the same). These secretive clauses, which you would never in your wildest dreams approve, mysteriously hide somewhere in the contracts you are signing with some dubious Lender. They have the same effect as when Brutus stabbed Caesar in the back.

The downfall of banking Giants like Lehman Brothers is a mere reflection of this betrayal, as they raced for more assets, bigger bonuses, and more power at the expense of the individual investor. This betrayal often seems to have started with a failure to put all of the facts on the table. As former Lehman executive Lawrence G. McDonald noted, "Have you ever noticed how, both in life and in corporations, one small piece of the economy with the truth often leads to full-blooded deceit and then a copper-bottomed southern-fried lie? And following right behind that lie, you usually find a real shady area, a kind of no-man's land where no one goes, not even in discussion with each other. We had one of those at Lehman. A deep, dark secret."[55] Such betrayal by the Giants generally starts out small, with such 'economy with the truth,' and expands into something much larger as one lie is built upon another lie, with the final betrayal of trust being the ultimate result.

How are we to respond to such betrayal by skilled Archers? The key to our response is to respond with the truth. Part of our role with organizations and as individuals is to fight such betrayal by presenting the truth, putting the facts on the table, and allowing these to speak for themselves. We are exhorted in John 8:32 by the words, "You shall know the truth, and the truth will make you free." Freedom comes to our own lives when we base facts on the truth and reveal what others would want to keep in the darkness.

An event that was to mirror my later life occurred when I was sixteen. I noticed the school bully antagonizing my school friends while we were playing rugby. I told my close friend that I was "unhappy about …'s bullying," but my friend told him another story.

A few days later, I received an invitation from this individual to a fighting 'duel' at his home, which was only a short distance from ours. I was worried, as I was up against a much stronger opponent than myself, but I was determined that I was not going to cower. When I arrived at the appointed time, my heart sank when I noticed that my friends, whom I had earlier tried to defend, were against me and had sided with this individual. I stood alone; nobody wanted to root for me; this was painful and shocking.

It took me a few weeks to lift my head at school due to the shame of having been beaten in this duel. But the confusion I felt that my friends had betrayed me was more heart-wrenching.

False accusations and betrayals are all circumstances that have occurred over the course of my life and which still follow me today. This is undoubtedly a painful, coded, and venomous arrow – a subject in which I have much experience.

Intimidation

Some banks are big culprits in making use of intimidation and threats to achieve their own will. Banks, by their very size and scale, are very intimidating in the potential power they have over individuals, organizations, and even nations. The debt book of JP Morgan Chase is several Trillion Dollars. Another example of the size and power of big banking giants is that in the nations of Ireland and Iceland, before 2008, their banking institutions had become so large that when the banks failed, the economies of those countries nearly collapsed.

Bank analyst Mike Mayo commented: "Large banks have enough clout to beat the living daylights out of anybody who gets in the way – politicians, the press, or analysts like me. They can effectively send you into exile, and they get their way more often than not."[56] Large institutions thus intimidate through their sheer size and scale, which often leaves the members of the public feeling totally at a loss.

Apart from their colossal size, big corporates also employ other intimidation tactics. For example, their attitude of competence, confidence, and even arrogance also causes those at odds with them to feel small and inferior and unable to respond, where clients feel that somewhere they have done something wrong. In a sense, because of their intimidating size, we often wrongly assume that they must be right all the time!

Acting superior: Many leaders of big corporates sadly have the attitude superiority. Part of this is because of their sheer scale. They do hold great power and regard themselves as superior to the rest of us dregs of society. "A major reason for the success of bank lobbying is that banking has a certain mystique,"[57] wrote Admati and Hellwig. "Anyone who questions that mystique and the claims that are made is at risk of being declared incompetent to participate in the discussion. Many of the claims made by leading bankers and banking experts actually have as much substance as the emperor's 'clothes' in the Hans Christian Andersen story *The Emperor's New Clothes*. However, most people do not challenge these claims, and the claims have an impact on policy. The specialists' pretense of competence and confidence is too intimidating. Even people who know better fail to speak up. The emperor may be naked, but he continues his parade without being challenged about his attire."[58]

Threatening intimidation: Another tactic of intimidation is the threat of legal action should you step out of line. This threat of legal action is made all the more intimidating by the fact that Banks have the finances to draw in large corporate law firms to fight their case, while those battling them often do not have the financial resources to acquire such high-level professional counsel.

In a sense, the Masters become intoxicated by their power. Fyodor Dostoyevsky noted, "Whoever has experienced the power and the unrestrained ability to humiliate another human being automatically loses his own sensations. Tyranny is a habit; it has its own organic life, and it finally develops into a disease. The habit can kill and coarsen the very best man or woman to the level of a beast. Blood and power intoxicate ... the return of the human dignity, repentance, and regeneration becomes almost impossible."[59]

Exercising power to seize assets: To make matters worse, it is within the power of Bankers to take away property, furniture, and other assets from the individual they are threatening. These threats generate fear, insecurity, and defenselessness. This often leads to a paralysis of action with the result that, in many cases, the Banks win without even stepping onto the battlefield. The intimidating complexity of the issues, including complex jargon, long and complicated legal documents, and huge amounts of paperwork, adds to this implicit and explicit intimidation.

How can we respond to these threats and practices of intimidation? My simple answer is this: Intimacy with God removes the fear of man. Righteousness prevails over unrighteousness, and it would only be a matter of time before intimidation tactics fail.

Complexity

Eric Daniels, former CEO of the UK's Lloyds Bank, when asked whether the banks were too big, replied, "I don't think it's a big-ness issue; it's a complexity issue." Indeed, one of the key weapons of Banks is complexity. It is debatable whether such complexity is purposeful, done to confuse and intimidate, or whether this is the result of the complex legislative requirements that banks are required to uphold. This complexity exists at two basic levels: (1) on the level of the structure and products of the institutions themselves, and (2) the complexity of processes, documents, and contracts within these institutions.

On an organizational level, big corporates are incredibly complex. The consulting firm *Simplicity* undertook a study in which they looked at the top 200 organizations in the Forbes Global 500. This study found that, on average, the world's largest companies are wasting 10.2% of their annual profits, or $1.2

billion each, due to value-destructive 'complexity.' As the study noted, "This proves that many companies are now too complex to perform at their best and are becoming slower to react to changing economic and competitive forces."[60]

There has been much debate in the media about whether some of the multinational banks are now 'too big to fail' as their failure could have global consequences. However, it's no longer a question of 'too big to fail'; rather, the danger today is that financial institutions are becoming 'too big to understand' and thus need to be simplified. There is also the complexity of the processes and products offered by big corporations, including the documentation generally forming part of this process.

Such complexity, although a coded arrow used by some institutions, appears to have backfired against them and has now become not just a challenge for those they are supposed to serve but for these institutions as well. The result is that some institutions are trying to engender greater simplicity to help them cope.

Most credit card agreements are unreadable to most adults, and they are generally at a reading level most can't understand. According to Roy Peter Clark, an expert on writing and a senior scholar at the Poynter Institute in St. Petersburg, Florida said: "Credit card contracts and other such documents are written in dense prose for a reason: So that the customer will NOT be able to understand it … I don't think their writing strategies are accidental, the collateral damage of a bureaucratic mindset. I think those writers know exactly what they are doing."[61] Banks inherently know the impact of what they are writing because the logic is quite simple: *a complex document is easier for a bank to defend in court*.

Banks often argue that commercial contracts are so complicated because of the legal requirements concerning what needs to be included. Nonsense, if the functionality of a more complex tool like an iPad can be simplified for use by the masses, then commercial contracts can be simplified for use by the masses.

I am experienced in economics, mathematics, accounting, law, and marketplace codes, and I have difficulty understanding most contracts provided by Banks. Although understanding is important, fair consumer protection is more important because what good does a short, understandable contract serve if the embedded purpose is that only one party wins in the deal?

How should we respond to such complexity? It's a difficult question, but make sure at least that complex language or legal jargon does not intimidate you.

Pride and Haughtiness

A culture of arrogance or general haughtiness seems to pervade the culture of those in power in the marketplace. Owing to the various arrows in the Big Boys' quiver and their immense power, they generally look down on the common person, and any small organization stepping into their domain is made to feel grossly inferior.

Although corporates have been working to change this culture (but it is certainly not at the top of their agenda), the public, in general, is still impacted by haughty attitudes and continues to be made to feel inferior. These feelings of inferiority are created through the attitude of many CEOs ("We are powerful;" "We are doing you a favor;" "You are a small fish in a large ocean"); through the scale and opulence of their office buildings ("Look what we have created;" "Look how much wealth we have;" "Look at how much power we have"); through titles and dress ("President;" "CEO," "Armani suits") through to the complexity of the products and the organization.

In the Middle Ages, priests were revered as they were the doorkeepers to the spiritual (standing between lowly humans and God). These days, CEO's are revered as they stand between lowly individuals and their success or happiness. On my own journey with the Titans, I experienced this haughtiness and pride in a myriad of ways. I was kept waiting for appointed meetings so that they could demonstrate their power over me; I was threatened by the size and complexity of those standing against me; I was belittled by harsh words and ungrounded criticism, and I was often made to feel like a slave.

How should we respond? Proverbs 16:18 cautions that "Pride goes before destruction and a haughty spirit before a fall." So, just walk away and dust the dirt off. Booker T. Washington, an African-American educator and author, left us with this thought: "Success is to be measured not so much by the position that one has reached in life as by the obstacles which he has overcome."

Mobbing

Then there is the highly poisonous coded arrow known as 'mobbing.' Dr Janice Harper, an expert anthropologist specializing in organizational cultures and warfare and a mobbing victim herself, wrote an excellent book on the subject. Dr Harper refers to *mobbing* as a 'gentle genocide,' saying:

> *"Group bullying runs amok where you are shunned, sabotaged, and put through the system with a series of bad reviews, passed opportunities, warnings, gossip, and accusations that often lead to investigations and inquisitions that can ultimately destroy your career."*[62]

In the book *Mobbing: Emotional Abuse in the American Workplace*, the authors identify mobbing as a particular type of bullying that is not as apparent as most, defining it as "... an emotional assault. It begins when an individual becomes the target of disrespectful and harmful behavior. Through innuendo, rumors, and public discrediting, a hostile environment is created in which one individual gathers others to willingly, or unwillingly, participate in continuous malevolent actions to force a person out of the workplace."[63]

Mobbing is group aggression, and it is distinct from bullying, which is more one-on-one. Mobbing does not just involve overt bullies, it can also include previously supportive, friendly, and non-aggressive individuals who have suddenly been influenced to view you as a threat. There is also a difference between warfare and mobbing because the former is the structured waging of violence of a group against another group, whereas mobbing is the structured antagonism of a group against an individual.

With mobbing, there is often a Chieftain involved who leads the charge by enlisting the support of an alpha or assassinator, who befriends your clients, colleagues, and friends with the sole objective of sullying your reputation with false accusations to create an evil filter through which others will view you in the future. In this way, alphas, who wish to be in the good books of the Chieftain, communicate to their organized members to justify their attacks against you 'for the good of everyone.' Anyone, competent or incompetent, right or wrong, can be mobbed.

Quite alarmingly, is that research has discovered that "when people behave in groups, their animal nature will almost always prevail over their personal nature [or their belief system]. Those who defy the group to defend another under attack are rare, and they are usually not the people we expect they will be."[64] Because animal behavior is prevalent, what individuals in groups actually believe to be fact has far less to do with truth but more to do with how others in the group are behaving. Interestingly:

A type of mobbing can start and gain momentum in this way:

1. at the outset, an individual or target is marked in a group or community as different, i.e., religion, set of beliefs, accent, talent, just different in the opinion of the group; then

2. you rub up a Chieftain the wrong way, which

3. confirms the innate feeling amongst the group that "you're not one of us"; painfully now

4. your behavior is more aggressively observed, and friction has ignited some smoke (gossip);

5. this gossip gains momentum, and passive observers join the group until animal instincts gain prevalence;

6. the gossip turns into facts (a fire has ignited), and the untruths start taking a life of their own, which leads to

7. false reports being made about your conduct so that

8. your friends and associates can lead the charge to discredit you, which justifies

9. society to be enraged by your actions (because your friends and colleagues have turned on you), which leads

10. to multiple group pecking.

Interestingly are the findings of Dr Konrad Lorenz, an Austrian zoologist, who, after watching the behavior of birds, could explain how mobbing could progress from the actions of an alpha bully to a venomous mob of people gone stark crazy.

Dr Lorenz observed that when a lone and unfamiliar bird strays into the territory of a group of birds, other birds will join in and circle the intruder, swooping and swooning, striking the intruder repeatedly with hard, swift blows (false accusations are often spread). These blows are not lethal at first, but only a fear tactic (the accusations are initially not serious, but eventually become more bizarre). If the intruder remains, the blows will increase until the intruder is slightly injured. The attacking birds will fly off momentarily but then return, watching, following, and encircling the injured bird. If the victim still does not leave, the birds will become more aggressive, swooping down again, grazing, drawing blood, retreating, and circling continuously until more onlookers gather who themselves turn into aggressors until the victim is severely injured from the blows.[65]

For those few readers who understand what mobbing and bullying are about, no further explanation is needed. For those who do not understand, no adequate explanation is possible.

Press in

As we have reviewed the coded arrows employed in the marketplace, it is important to realize that what the Aggressors are trying to achieve with their multitude of arrows is to remove the competition or keep us subject to the system. Our best defense against these arrows is to continue to press into those things burning on our hearts, walking wisely and circumspectly, seeking the wisdom of God, but not being ignorant of the dangers we face.

We need to choose to rise above these trying circumstances to allow what is right and true to define who we are and where we are going. Proverbs 11:2,3 - "When pride comes, then comes disgrace, but with humility comes wisdom. The integrity of the upright guides them, but the unfaithful are destroyed by their duplicity."

On a lighter note, if you want to avoid becoming a corporate villain, treat them like a particularly irritating customer: turn off read receipts, keep your replies vague, and disappear into the depths of their own bureaucratic maze. Then, when they eventually send a legal demand because you didn't cater to their every whim, simply respond that it's just you and your two parrots (your advisors). This tends to confuse their imaginative minds - after all, no one wants to tangle with your mystery team.

CHAPTER 5
TECHNIQUES OF CONFLICT

"Behold, I send you out as sheep in the midst of wolves.
Therefore, be wise as serpents and harmless as doves."

(Matthew 10:16)

The Nature of the Battle

Conflict or war is, by nature, a terrible experience. War and deep conflict are a formidable experience that shapes individuals for the rest of their lives, because marketplace conflict, like war, is very invasive. It affects the physical body, the emotions, and it affects our minds as it touches us to the very core, our soul.

The list below summarizes some of the emotions faced during the conflict, including examples from some more modern wars:

o   *Battle weary.* Soldiers battled the darkness, smell, dirt, poor sanitation, lack of nutritious food, and other deprivations of war.

o   *Fear.* A soldier would have faced a daily war in body and mind, fearful of the weapons being used against him, fearful of the unknown, fearful of what the day ahead would bring, and, ultimately, fearful of dying like his comrades around him.

o   *Hopelessness.* Trench warfare mostly lasted for years. Soldiers stuck in the mud and smell of war would have battled hopelessness as months went by with no glimmer on the horizon of an end to it.

o   *Disconnected from reality.* The reality for the soldier was about the battle being fought, so soldiers often felt very disconnected from the rest of life. Soldiers would journey back home from the front line, where the emotional turmoil continued. It was often difficult for them to understand how normal life could continue while they dealt with the realities of war.

o   *Loneliness and isolation.* Soldiers stuck endlessly in the trenches, facing those daily hardships, experienced loneliness and disconnection. Their families back home could never comprehend what they were experiencing.

o   *Loss of identity.* Soldiers lost a sense of who they were. The battles became all-encompassing and the only focus, with the result that soldiers lost touch with the reality of their pre-war identity. In addition, their experiences during the war shaped a new persona, often one they could not grasp or adequately understand themselves.

o   *Alienation from others.* As soldiers cannot easily express the horrors of the battles they have faced (and the continuing war waging in their minds), they often feel alienated from others.

Marketplace participants deep in conflict often find themselves stuck in a vortex and encounter a similar range of emotions. Not only are they often kept with constant threats, perhaps in the darkness of mind, surrounded by impenetrable walls that seem to press in on them, but they also battle many of the emotions touched on above: battle weary, fighting fear, hopelessness, loss of identity, feeling disconnected from reality, and facing real loneliness and isolation.

Experience in the Trenches

True marketplace conflict does more than test an individual - it shapes him. It forges an identity in the heat of the struggle and casts a long shadow over what his future self may become. I have lived through these conflicts. At times, it felt as though I had been cast adrift in a sea of darkness, hemmed in by towering walls that closed in from every side. I fought hard against the financial risks that threatened my assets, growing weary in a way that surprised me, certainly no stranger to battle.

Often, in marketplace conflict, we are dwarfed by weapons far greater than we have in our arsenal. In this kind of battle, there is no true respite. The conflict walks beside you like a persistent shadow, denying rest. Only those who have endured it firsthand can truly grasp the emotional, physical, spiritual, and mental toll it exacts in the trenches of the marketplace.

Like a soldier crouched in the trenches, each of us faces a critical choice: surrender and retreat to a quiet corner of the world or rise with purpose and conviction, ready to contend for what is right and true. In every choice lies deeper spiritual crossroads — hatred or love, vengeance or forgiveness. I hope that this book can be an additional aid in that journey, designed to help you keep hold of your soul with integrity intact, for it is in that unwavering integrity that true peace is found, not the mere absence of conflict, but with the presence of divine clarity.

The biblical Paul and Silas, when they were in prison, also faced these emotions, and they too made a choice about their response. Imprisoned for preaching the life and hope of Jesus in the Jewish temple, the Bible aptly reflects their response, "Having received such a charge, he [the jailer] put them into the inner prison and fastened their feet in the stocks. But at midnight, Paul and Silas were praying and singing hymns to God, and the prisoners were listening to them."[66] The end result was that the prison was shaken by an earthquake, they were released, and their jailer and his whole family became Christians. These two men chose a godly response to their circumstances, as should we as we face these emotions.

Statesman Nelson Mandela, in a letter to his wife, wrote: "No axe is sharp enough to cut the soul of a sinner who keeps on trying, one armed with the hope that he will rise in the end."[67] Martin Luther, the great reformer of the church in the 16th century, noted a similar sentiment as he stood before his accusers at the Diet of Worms in 1521, "I cannot and will not recant anything, for to go against conscience is neither right nor safe. Here I stand; I can do no other, so help me God."

This Chapter is like a war manual, but only to be considered as a defense against the wiles of the Chieftains and their companions, because the mindset of the Christian is to seek peace, but sometimes war is inevitable. Biblical evidence from the book of Nehemiah is clear: with one hand, the builders of the wall worked at construction, and with the other held a weapon.

The Illusion

Rodney Buchanan aptly describes the workings of the illusionist or magician:

> "*The trick of the illusionist is to use sleight-of-hand to get you to look at one thing while he is doing something else. He makes you think one thing is happening when something else is actually going on. He makes you think that what you see is real while he is hiding what is really happening. To state it briefly, what appears to be is not what is.*" [68]

That, in essence, is what has happened in Psalm 73. Asaph, who wrote Psalm 73, was looking at all the wrong things. The ancient magician, Lucifer, had the psalmist's eyes looking at what he wanted him to see, aimed at discouraging and depressing Asaph. Lucifer did not want Asaph to see what God was doing, so he used a sleight of hand to distract him to focus only on the prosperity of the wicked. As a result of the illusion, Asaph's feet almost slipped, and he nearly lost his foothold to discouragement and defeat.

Asaph mused: "For there are no pangs in their [the wealthy and arrogant] death, but their strength is firm. They are not in trouble like other men, nor are they plagued like other men. Therefore, pride serves as their necklace; violence covers them like a garment. Their eyes bulge with abundance; They have more than heart could wish."[69]

This was the same complaint that the prophet Jeremiah had when he wrote: "Righteous are You, O LORD, when I plead with You; Yet let me talk with You about Your judgments. Why does the way of the wicked prosper? Why are those happy who deal so treacherously?"[70] But this is the trick of the illusionist, of the Chieftain. He diverts your attention with his actions to keep you from seeing what is really going on.

Refuse to Believe the Illusion

Many who witnessed illusionist David Copperfield make the Statue of Liberty vanish genuinely believed it was gone. Of course, it would be foolish to think someone had actually removed such an iconic monument — yet the power of illusion is undeniable.

And just as audiences fall for magic tricks, many people fall for the illusion that what they see in the marketplace is reality. They believe power, wealth, and dominance are immovable truths. But often, what seems to prevail is merely a shadow play — a deceptive force cloaked in authority and control. There are indeed great forces of good in this world, but malice can often appear to be the dominant power. The marketplace is rife with Chieftains who wield their financial influence like a magician's wand, crafting illusions of control, superiority, and inevitability.

These figures aim to break your spirit through discouragement. Their tactics whisper lies into your soul: "I am winning. I am the master of your life. There is nothing you can do. Pay what I demand. Surrender your story, or I will cut you off." When you start to believe that evil is permanent and power is untouchable, the illusion has done its work.

Consider William Wilberforce, who fought tirelessly for the abolition of slavery in Britain. The political machinery he faced was formidable, unmoved by his pleas. Discouragement nearly silenced him — until a letter from his dying friend John Wesley reignited his fire. From his deathbed, Wesley wrote, "Unless God has raised you up for this very thing, you will be worn out by the opposition of men and devils. But if God be for you, who can be against you? Are all of them stronger than God? Oh, be not weary of well-doing! Go on, in the name of God and in the power of His might, till even American slavery shall vanish away before it."

Wesley died six days later. Wilberforce pressed on — not for six months or six years, but for another forty-five years — and slavery was finally abolished in England just three days before his own passing.

Wilberforce refused to believe that evil was invincible. So must you. The illusion of dominance must be challenged, especially in a marketplace that too often mirrors modern-day slavery in its exploitative tactics. There is a better way, and it begins with faith that good, guided by divine power, can and will prevail.

The Art of Conflict

In the marketplace, serious conflict, a type of war, may arise against you personally (as a worker in a company) or against your company (as an owner of a company). I have learned the best conflict strategies from the bible, my father, and from my own experience, but also valuable lessons on the art of engaging in conflict can be gleaned by studying principles from successful military generals.[71]

Previously, I decoded marketplace codes. Now, I present some codes of our own:

Code # 1: Underestimation

I have placed this war strategy at the top of my list because it is a very effective weapon against the proud and arrogant Chieftains and their accomplices. Pretend inferiority and thereby encourage their arrogance. Their arrogance is most certainly their weakness. Eliminate their actions by this Achilles' heel.

This arrogance is a severe weakness that will lead to their downfall. Proverbs 16:18 is clear: "Pride goes before destruction and a haughty spirit before a fall."

I remember how I was once summoned by a Chieftain and his team (this was a frequent event for me) and, sitting in front of them at their intimidating offices, was told how useless I was and how they were going to shut down my business. I silently prayed, and I sensed a still, small voice guiding me to "look behind me."

In my mind's eye, I saw this cavalry of horses and soldiers in the boardroom, and thinking that the Chieftain had also seen this sight and being so excited that my prayer had brought in the cavalry, my reply to the Chieftain and his small cavalry was, "You - and Who?" Clearly, I should have been more discreet with my words because a flame of fire from the Chieftain scorched my hair.

Code # 2: Stealth Strategy

It's easy to observe the tactics of others that may make them overcome, but don't forget that they will employ an overarching strategy to guide their tactics. What worked for others will not necessarily work for you. Chieftains don't always use the same tactics on everyone. No, they are the 'Masters of illusion,' so in order for you to prevail over your Chieftains, set out an unassailable strategy from which your victory will evolve.

Our family business's stealth strategy has always been prayer and active observance, and if we humbled ourselves before our Lord, He would fight the war on our behalf. Faith and works must walk side by side. As my father observed, I studied the enemy's code. Our stealth was in their surprise - they never imagined we had the intellect. While they laced their words with venom, we responded with an embrace.

Code # 3: Believe in Yourself & Your Team

It is unwise for a military commander to enter into battle without an expectation of winning. If you don't believe you can win, you won't. Belief in yourself, faith in your abilities, and faith in God (for the Christian) is a common thread amongst all successful entrepreneurs.

Chieftains will invade your space and enter your home with the arrogance that you are a lost cause, and they will make you feel like a lost cause. During my war years, many Chieftains taunted me nearly daily. The intimidation seemed overwhelming, but I focused on keeping possession of my soul in faith. I believed in Jesus, who saved me, Father God, who loved me, and in the Holy

Spirit, who empowered and comforted me. In that faith, I found my victory.

I recall the incident when I was asked to leave university because, in my first two years, I had such low grades (actually, it was not the low grades that my moderator was concerned about, but the fact that she did not like my personality). Because I took the battle back to the university and never retreated, God's grace enabled me to become the only student at the time to be awarded a Ph.D in the faculty of commerce.

Code # 4: Retain and Dismiss

Military commander Sun Tzu aptly recommends, "The general that hearkens to my counsel and acts upon it will conquer; let such a one be retained in command! The general that hearkens not to my counsel nor acts upon it will suffer defeat: let such a one be dismissed." [72]

When the wolf Chieftain attacks the shepherd, most of the sheep (employees or partners) will scatter. Trust me on this. The shepherd has to be skilled in both defending himself against the wolf and re-gathering the sheep. Probably the majority of your sheep will desert you when the wolf attacks. Many of those who remain will challenge and question your integrity as they will be asking themselves, "If there is smoke, there must be a fire." They forget to remember that "When there is blood (a malicious wound inflicted by a Chieftain), there are also sharks." Sun Tzu is correct;

116

promptly dismiss those who work against you, but retain and nurture those who are for you.

When BlackBerry, once the reigning chieftain of smartphones, faltered due to sluggish innovation (the general who did not hearken to counsel) and a delayed response (the general who did not act upon counsel) to touchscreen technology, competitors like Apple and Android makers quickly seized the opportunity. As BlackBerry's market share dwindled, these rivals swooped in like sharks, winning customers and taking control of the market.

Code # 5: Opportunities Multiply as They are Seized

Big opportunities often come gift-wrapped in unsuspecting packages. What looks small can often act as a springboard to something much greater, thereby taking on a domino effect, a chain reaction.

In the early days, Steve Jobs grew frustrated with Apple's tangled projects and internal conflicts. Yet, from a side endeavor, considered risky and unconventional, emerged the Macintosh, a compact and user-friendly computer. This unexpected venture transformed personal computing and solidified Apple's place in history.

I was once embroiled in a legal battle with my ex-business partners, who tried to convince the courts that I was a bad partner and that they deserved 100% of the company. I knew that my partners were motivated by greed and that their story was false.

After two years in the courts, my adversary had to change their attorneys, and when their files were sent by the old attorneys to the new attorneys, the address was incorrectly stated as that of my own attorneys' firm!

Most court cases work on the principle of full disclosure of all documents, so when my attorneys opened this incorrectly sent box of files ('big opportunities often come gift-wrapped in unsuspecting packages'), believing it was part of the information disclosure process, only to find the damaging information withheld by my assailants, and I won my case.

Code # 6: Investigate the Deception

Most warfare involved swaths of deception. Deception can be defined as deliberately causing someone to believe something that is not true, especially for personal gain.

There are numerous examples of the use of deception in war. Deception in wartime is usually achieved by creating or amplifying the fog of war by using psychological operations, visual deception, and information warfare. Deception works because if an enemy falls for the deception, is distracted, and places focus and resources elsewhere, he may lose confidence in his abilities once the deception is revealed. In addition, once deceived, the enemy may make the grave mistake of hesitating when the truth is revealed.

Deception is, however, not limited to wartime. Deception can lead to feelings of betrayal and distrust between partners. Deception is a deep and painful violation of relational norms and can irreparably harm a relationship.

People generally expect friends, partners, colleagues, and even strangers to be truthful in their dealings with one another. Deception serves to distort or omit the truth. Chieftains are experts at deception, as people enter into a relationship with another under the impression that their relationship is based on truth and on serving each other's best interests. Unfortunately, Chieftains clearly have their own best interests in mind and so end up not presenting the whole picture or walking in truth and transparency.

Although Chieftains use deception more generally in how they operate in life, we are called to walk in truth. The wolf is, unfortunately, a sharp-sighted, cunning creature that uses various means and strategies to preserve itself.

We need to ensure that we use all proper methods to preserve ourselves from the plans and deceptive schemes of men and not to expose ourselves to unnecessary danger, avoiding all snares and traps laid for us by the Chieftains. In being wise like the serpent, however, we are also called to be harmless as doves - free from cunning and violence while responding in humility and meekness.

Our role is to wisely and carefully interact with the Chieftains. We need to be aware of their very nature and thus walk with circumspection and caution. One of the deceptions that the Chieftains implement is confusion and complexity, especially with the nature of the contractual documentation that forms such a clear part of their world. Sign any document with your eyes wide open, and borrow a few more eyes where you can.

Code # 7: Look for Gaps in the Armory

Military Commander Sun Tzu exhorted us to: "Hold out baits to entice the enemy. Feign disorder and crush him." He explains this further by noting, "If he is secure at all points, be prepared for him. If he is in superior strength, evade him. If your opponent is of choleric temper, seek to irritate him. Pretend to be weak, that he may grow arrogant. If he is taking his ease, give him no rest. If his forces are united, separate them."

This principle illustrates that a good strategy is to surprise, to meet the enemy in a way that he is not expecting. The skill here is to be able to study your enemy with care, to recognize his strengths and weaknesses, and then to respond in a manner that he does not expect.

Chieftains are adept at living according to this principle. They intimidate you and make your position look tenuous by pressurizing you into signing long contracts that are written in complex language that you fail to comprehend. The length and complexity of these documents already make one feel in some way inferior to the Chieftains. Then, if you fail to meet your obligations in terms of this contract, they start to harass you with letters from law firms, who use their sheer size and financial weight to coerce you to meet their demands, where they might not even be able to make a real case, let alone win the battle in a court of law.

We can, however, defend ourselves against the Chieftains' attacks by looking for a gap in their defenses. We can use their perceived strength and our perceived weakness in our favor. For example, their very size makes maneuverability and lateral thinking more difficult, whereas smaller organizations do not have the associated bureaucracy in place and can consequently maneuver more easily and faster. I strongly negotiated one word in a lengthy bank contract, which saved our bacon, which I was able to legally argue successfully when maliciously attacked.

This leads to the famous story when Goliath challenges David, and instead of using the conventional weapon of a sword or a spear to do so, David uses a small slingshot to defeat Goliath.

Another example is the story of a small business that had signed surety on another Company's debts. The borrower entered bankruptcy from undue pressure exerted by the Lender, leaving the small business responsible for the $4.2 million surety owed to the aggressive bank. The bank then took this small business to court to retrieve the money. At a certain stage in the court proceedings, the court asked to see the original of the signed surety document. It then turned out that this document had been lost in the bank's internal mail while being sent from one branch to another. As a result, the entire court case fell apart.

Code # 8: Play at the Psyche

Sun Tzu advises, "If your opponent is of choleric temper, seek to irritate him. Pretend to be weak, that he may grow arrogant."

Study the character flaws of the Chieftains and play on their shortcomings. Your Chieftain could probably fall into the Dark Triad of character traits that include the self-obsession of narcissism or callous behavior. Know it, and play to their arrogance.

Malevolent leaders callously disregard the needs of others and are prepared to lie, bully, and cheat to cause harm to third parties. But the chink in their armor (their area of vulnerability) is that they are mostly poor managers who individually have a negative impact on many areas of their own organization. You will easily find friends in their organization who will sympathize with you.

Sonny Liston, a formidable and intimidating boxing heavyweight champion, was known for his aggression and quick temper. Muhammad Ali recognized that he couldn't overcome Liston through brute force alone. Instead, Ali employed psychological tactics - mocking him as "the big ugly bear," dancing around the ring, and taunting him during the fight - to provoke an emotional reaction. Aware that Liston's choleric nature made him vulnerable to losing composure, Ali exploited this weakness. The angrier Liston became, the wilder and more ineffective his attacks grew, allowing Ali to wear him down and ultimately secure victory.

Code # 9: Counter Overreliance on Intimidation

Relying heavily on intimidation, malicious attackers often neglect to consider how they'll respond if their target resists or exposes their bluff. Avoid escalating or responding emotionally. Bluffs often fall apart when they don't provoke the intended reaction.

Intimidation is a behavior that typically involves discouraging or forcing another person or group through the threat of harm. Some classic examples of intimidation are being aggressive, seeking vengeance, manipulation, or intentionally embarrassing another.

My eldest brother, Michael, is skilled at defusing volatile or intimidating situations. Honestly, it's quite comical but well executed. What he does is respond in the exact opposite way the opponent expects. While the individual anticipates us to start groveling, Michael instead approaches him and says something like, "I can see you're upset. Let me order a nice cappuccino, and we can enjoy this sunny day together. I believe tomorrow will be a better day for you."

By this point, the opponent has grown even more furious, letting out a few swear words, but the positive outcome is that he walks away from the conversation, and I get to enjoy his cappuccino.

Code # 10: Need to Know Information

As a father, part of my role is to protect my wife and children from elements in the world that would bring them harm or cause anxiety in their hearts. For example, whenever I was informed of malicious attacks on our businesses, if I had shared this with my children, they would have responded in fear and would have gone into the rest of the day and beyond with a deep insecurity growing in their hearts.

A vital part of a leader is to manage the information that is fed through to those following him, depending on their position, the relevance of the information to their role, the degree of trust he has in them, and whether they, in fact, need to know the information. This strategy, of course, is only relevant to private companies; listed and regulated companies have defined rules for information sharing.

The term 'need to know,' often used by government and military organizations, describes the restriction of access to data or information that is considered very sensitive. Only if such information is necessary for the conduct of one's official duties would it be made available. This provides a safeguard against vital information reaching the wrong people in the wrong way and/or at the wrong time.

In privately held businesses, it's prudent to limit the amount of information shared with others, especially to protect your company's intellectual property rights.

Code # 11: Surprise where the Enemy is Unprepared

You have a strong advantage when you are defending yourself against arrogant adversaries. They often believe "they've got you cornered," and since this is often the case, you must prepare well, be creative, and then surprise them.

I was taught early on not to view others as enemies. So, when I refer to an 'adversary' here, I mean someone who has chosen to see me as theirs. With that clarification, I should say, I always kept my unique ability to decode under wraps, shared only with friends.

I could assess someone's posture, mindset, and intentions (whether genuine or harmful), far quicker than most, giving me the clarity to walk away from deals when necessary. Many were caught off guard, surprised that I possessed any talent at all. But one by one, those with hidden agendas began to pull back and fall in line, once they realized I was not someone to be trifled with.

Though first appearing as a passive investor in Twitter, Elon Musk quickly revealed himself as a takeover contender. Caught off guard, Twitter's leadership found the company swept into new ownership, marked by sweeping changes. Swift and unexpected financial maneuvers can outflank slower, less agile enterprises.

Code # 12: Exacerbate the Urgency

The term "exacerbate the urgency" refers to making the sense of urgency of a matter stronger or more severe. If you recognize the relevance of the science of psychology, your business journey will be a more comfortable one.

We need to start by understanding why psychology and business are inextricably linked. In 2002, Princeton University psychologist Daniel Kahneman was awarded the Nobel Memorial Prize in Economic Sciences for his ground-breaking work in applying psychological insights to economic theory.[73] Together with an associate, he developed the economic model known as prospect theory (also discussed in chapter 1) to better explain analogous economic behavior that's difficult to account for with traditional models.

As previously discussed, prospect theory suggests that people look at gains and losses differently and, as such, will base decisions on perceived gains rather than on perceived losses. In other words, if an individual is given two equal choices, one based on possible gains and the other on possible losses, he will choose the former.

Chieftains with harmful intent are often more focused on the potential losses they might suffer from an attack than the possible gains. By intensifying their perception of the risks and urgency of those losses, you can cause them to hesitate and make poor strategic decisions, giving you the upper hand in the duel.

Code # 13: Reply in Shakespearean English

While the advice may appear comical at first glance, the underlying strategy is surprisingly effective. I stayed 14 years in Shakespeare's hometown, Stratford-upon-Avon, so I know something about this remarkable playwright.

Malicious actors often scrutinize your profile and may, as example, perceive you as a person with a Christian worldview. From that, they might most likely form a prejudiced view - labeling you as a hypocrite, dishonest, idiot, or overly zealous - and question your right to challenge what they see as their flawless judgment of any situation.

By answering in the tongue of Shakespeare, thou dost make plain unto thine adversary that thou art wise to their deeds, possesseth wit, and canst unravel their enigmatical weapon. Such a missive, though cloaked in flourish, shall be well perceived by keen merchants and leave them pondering at the depth of thy discernment.

To my fellow Christians who believe it wise to avoid arrogance, I agree. Yet, when I find myself in the pigsty, I must place an apple in the pig's mouth - lest it turn and bite me on the neck. In Shakespearean terms: In sooth, thou dost parry their assault with wit and tempered grace, thus showing thou art no fool to be trifled with, yet wielding not the sword of open wrath. That apple, thy wise reply, is placed in yonder swine's mouth, that it might gnash not nor gain dominion o'er thee.

Code # 14: Do not be Quickly Provoked

Ecclesiastes 7:9 aptly says, "Do not hasten in your spirit to be angry, for anger rests in the bosom of fools."

Chieftains who are quick to attack pursue their self-centered business goals without feeling the pangs of guilt. Taken from the science of psychology, the fruit of such self-centeredness is irresponsibility, impulsivity, and a parasitic lifestyle, amongst others.

We need to thoroughly analyze our opponents to uncover their weaknesses. Maintain your composure and avoid reacting hastily - this will increase the chance that your opponent, likely driven by impulse and anger, will make reckless errors you can exploit.

I recall a particularly challenging client who became angry after not receiving a full refund for a late cancellation at one of our hotels. She responded by posting numerous harsh reviews on online travel sites, criticizing even the smallest issues. Despite the provocation, the hotel staff remained composed. However, the guest escalated the situation by visiting the hotel in person to vent her frustration. She caused a scene at the reception desk, yelling loudly - an incident that was captured on the hotel's security cameras. The staff calmly informed her that her behavior had been recorded, and after that, the hotel never heard from her again.

Code # 15: Be Quiet

In conflict, you place yourself at a significant advantage by being quiet. Listen five times as much as you speak. This silence gives you the space to gather information, observe the Chieftain's careless surmising, maintain control, formulate a response, and avoid negative reactive rebuttals. Proverbs 17:27-28 says that wisdom can be found in restraint and silence.

During World War II, the Germans relied on the Enigma machine to encrypt military communications, confident in its impenetrability. British codebreakers eventually decoded Enigma's secrets, but rather than reacting to every intercepted message, they often chose silence. Acting too openly would have alerted the Germans to the breach, likely prompting a change in their encryption and forfeiting the strategic edge.

When you are not actively communicating, you become the best observer; your brain is given the opportunity to be creative from the study of the Bible, which must become to you a lamp to your feet and a light to your path to cross the treacherous terrain.

Admittedly, staying silent can be difficult; however, silence is a powerful and often underestimated asset in effective business management. It allows us to grasp not only what is spoken, but also what is left unsaid. In many cases, silence paves the way to uncovering the truth more easily.

Code # 16: Prioritize Questions over Responses

In conflict situations, take the initiative by prioritizing thoughtful questions over direct responses. Ensure your questions are intellectually framed to encourage constructive dialogue. This strategy holds multiple advantages: while your adversary may take issue with your personality, he will find it difficult to challenge your intellect and will think twice before attempting to deceive you. Below are two practical examples of such questions:

Your boss angrily asks, "why 'you' have not applied your full marketing budget?" with your suggested counter reply, "the product 'I' am developing is designed to be the best in its class, do you want me to spend my budget on product innovation or marketing?"

I once read about a true and amusing exchange between the company board of a car manufacturer and their strategy consultant. When the board asked how much budget should be allocated to electric vehicle development, the consultant responded with a clever question of his own: "How much clean air does the consumer want?"

Code # 17: Pay for Lunch

The reader will not like this advice, but it works. If the Chieftain and his accomplices have maneuvered a trap in a contract or a trap for you in another avenue, thereby forcing you to give up an item, and when they come and collect the asset, they will brazenly also require you to pay for the transport, their time, and their lunch.

You may wonder (and fret), "Why do they go this far to nail me?" Because in their mind, you deserve this treatment, and now they must go out of their way to arrange for the transport of your item to their sheds (they would have preferred that you delivered the item to them personally). Do not hesitate, do not fret, pay these costs.

This payment will serve as your seed investment when everything illicitly taken from you will need to be returned tenfold or even a hundredfold. A person of true faith does things in the opposite direction. Biblical evidence of this principle is found in Jeremiah 12.

The prophet Jeremiah dreams that someone will come and offer him the chance to purchase a field. However, the timing of this land purchase makes no financial sense because, at the time, the entire nation of Israel was in exile, away from the Promised Land. Jeremiah obeys God's direction and buys the field, doubling down on God's promise to return the Israelites from exile.

Code # 18: Keep Smiling

At the time of writing this book, my father is 93 years old. I'm honored that both my parents live with my family, and my father often reminds me of the undertaking I made to him when he entrusted me with a leadership role: to read the Bible, not fly business class, avoid buying a fancy car, and always to smile.

It's the last point that I want to emphasize here. My paternal grandmother was French, and my paternal grandfather was of Lebanese-French descent. He passed away when my father was still very young, so my father was raised by his mother in the French tradition. The French have a natural charm, smiling effortlessly and speaking with that beautiful accent, so I came to understand all too well why the smile was so important to my father. In fact, the charm of the French is so endearing that I have written a large part of this book in Paris.

A genuine, heartfelt smile can be a powerful tool for defusing anger and disarming even the most hostile person. Statesman Nelson Mandela, known for his warm, reassuring smile, often used it to lower the guard of even the most hostile opponents. In early meetings with former apartheid leaders, his calm demeanor and friendly smile helped open doors to dialogue that once seemed impossible. A sincere smile signals grace, calmness, and a willingness to engage in a diplomatic manner.

Code # 19: Stand for Values

According to Sun Tzu, "(The) Commander [must] stand for the virtues of wisdom, sincerity, benevolence, courage, and strictness."

Only the last of these virtues, i.e., 'strictness,' can safely be attributed to Chieftains; the others are foreign to them, and your values will confuse them. Keeping Chieftains puzzled is always a good strategy, but the main reason you need to stand for values is that it attracts the blessings of God upon your life, and you sure will need them.

In fact, research by the Barrett Values Center,[74] which studied 2,000 organizations across 60 countries, demonstrated that "values-driven organizations are the most successful organizations on the planet."

The reasons for this are that in the private sector, values and behavior drive culture. Culture drives employee fulfillment, and employee fulfillment drives customer satisfaction. Customer satisfaction drives shareholder value and business success. As an individual and as an organization, guided by your values ensures that you not only do not end up fighting battles that you should not be fighting, but also ensure that even during the battles, you can stand and keep fighting.

Code # 20: Banish Fear

Fear has no place in the life of a Christian, including in their conduct within the marketplace. When we neglect to honor Christ through steadfast faith, our constant worries and fears become a form of dishonor to Him and weaken our witness and destroy our businesses. Fear spreads like wildfire - just a small spark can ignite a blaze that consumes everything in its path.

When fear takes root within, it easily finds fuel from outside sources as well. It may feed on weak cash flow, memories of the past, or anxieties about the future. Even those who trust in God can sometimes become overwhelmed by fear and distress over everyday business situations - matters they should, through faith, either disregard or rise above. Some people are especially prone to fear, perceiving danger where none exists. There are even those who seem to have a sorrowful talent for imagining hardships. And when the Lord has not sent them a trial, they create one for themselves.

My antagonists often labelled my banishment of fear as "presumption" and were astonished that anyone could place such confidence in God. Yet, to me, unbelief carries far more presumption than faith ever could. Surely, it is a gross error for a child to doubt his father's word - there's no arrogance in a child trusting what his father says; that's simply his duty. In the same way, for me to embrace the plain promise of a faithful and loving God, and to believe it true despite my dangerous circumstances, is by no means arrogance or pride, but rather faith in action.

Isaiah 41:10 commands, "Fear not, for I am with you; Be not dismayed, for I am your God." This verse is absolute and unconditional - we are not to fear in any circumstance. Period.

Code # 21: Keep True Perspective

We give far too much importance to our professions, and we start to idolize the marketplace, sinning thereby in our attitudes. We believe that a crisis in our profession is fatal for our continued survival when, in fact, as members of the body of Christ, any crisis is only a scratch on our toenails. You may be shaking your head at me for making this statement, but you then forget that it is not my opinion that counts; only truth prevails, which is this:

Acts 5:31 states that God has exalted Jesus to His right hand. As Christians are one with Christ, we are members of His body as Scripture records, and therefore His exaltation is our protection. Only Jesus sits at God's right hand; only the Triune God is divine. Revelation 19:12 goes further and reveals that Jesus has many crowns on His head.

These crowns symbolize Jesus' complete authority and victory over all powers and kingdoms, and this authority and power extend to the marketplace. The crowns (plural) also symbolize that Jesus is not content with having a crown only for Himself but shares His many crowns with His family, so we too can overcome. I rest my point; a marketplace crisis should be viewed with true perspective, nothing more, and you will recover your peace.

Wisdom to Overcome

I suggested numerous codes to use in business conflicts, which will assist in the battle against unfair practices. There is also wisdom to be found in the secular, for all people are made in the image of God, and so they are also wisely able to make sense of life. But this is not to say that they have enough sense to make the most of life. The world's wisdom will always fall short, for it lacks eternal perspective.

Beyond these coded techniques mentioned, the most effective is a biblical mindset of wisdom. Proverbial truth reminds us that "the Lord gives wisdom... When wisdom enters your heart, and knowledge is pleasant to your soul, discretion will preserve you; understanding will keep you, to deliver you from the way of evil, from the man who speaks perverse things."[75]

At the outset, honor God in adversity; everything else can be neglected, but not bible study, not prayer, not praise, not worship. Matthew 4:4 - "Man shall not live by bread alone, but by every word that proceeds from the mouth of God." I reflect on this in more detail in the last Chapter.

Wisdom sees the total problem or issue from God's perspective. It takes an eternal look and doesn't just focus on immediate trials and present pain. Rather, wisdom combined with knowledge and understanding gives those who fear God a way to not only persevere but also to overcome trials and barriers.

CHAPTER 6
VALLEY OF ADVERSITY

"The spirit of a man will sustain him in sickness,

But who can bear a broken spirit?"

(Proverbs 18:14)

End Game

The preamble to this book alluded to the fact that the marketplace is a Game of Thrones. This game is not a rugby match where physical injury is the order of the day, and admittedly, injuries sustained in many sports are of a serious nature.

Rather, injuries sustained in the marketplace are much more serious, as this Proverb suggests, that while a strong spirit can sustain physical sickness or injuries, a broken or wounded spirit is much harder to bear. The profound, harmful impact of emotional pain and distress cannot be overemphasized.

I have decoded in the previous Chapters; now, this Chapter deals with the end game of negative marketplace codes, leading marketplace participants to the 'valley of adversity,' with most succumbing to the effects of a 'broken spirit.' Here, decoding is not required; we rather venture into the nature of this valley and our escape from it.

Mental and emotional well-being become significant factors in marketplace success, in most cases, sadly neglected by marketplace participants because they have not identified these strange codes, and neither understand the impact negative codes have on the spirit.

While physical health is essential for business success, a strong spirit is vital because it is (i) needed to sustain good health and (ii) the energy for the treacherous mountain climb, which I term in this book the "Everest Mountain of Thrones." A broken spirit leads to hopelessness, despair, depression, loss of motivation, and, if not managed, more serious mental illnesses, hospitalization, and, in some cases, death.

The previous chapters have led us to the knowledge that the Everest Mountain of Thrones cannot be reached without traversing the 'valley of adversity.' Bad news to all climbers who wish to reach the top of the Everest Mountain of Thrones: this very dangerous and emotionally taxing valley needs to be crossed.

I am reminded by the exhortation in Acts 14:22: "We must, through many tribulations, enter the kingdom of God." Charles Spurgeon said, "It is ordained of old that the cross of trouble should be engraved on every vessel of mercy, as the royal mark whereby the King's vessels of honor are distinguished."[76] My privileged exposure to the world's financial system has taught me that the system is meticulously designed to attempt to bring you down and keep you down; it craftily sabotages God's plan for your life.

I agree with Kay Arthur when she states in her book, *When the Hurt Runs Deep*, that "deep, exhausting, unrelenting, unrelieved hurt can bring you to the end of yourself. And that's the very best place to be."[77] Steven Furtick, in his book *Greater,* put it wonderfully, "God initiates the biggest changes in our lives through the smallest starts."[78]

The reader may well think to himself at this juncture, "What if the market participant deserved this fate through his/her own erroneous actions?" That is, of course, possible, but the point being made here is that the vast majority of people find themselves in this valley regardless of their best and sincere efforts. Let's look at this from another angle: if someone falls off a cliff due to their own mistake, would you refuse to help them heal unless you could first prove they were not negligent in any shape or form?

I am reminded of the caution from Hosea 4:6 - "My people are destroyed for lack of knowledge." You are now equipped with the knowledge that you need to prepare yourself for the attack to break your spirit. Be encouraged: the great news from 1 Corinthians 10:13:

"No temptation has overtaken you except such as is common to man, but God is faithful, who will not allow you to be tempted beyond what you are able, but with the temptation will also make the way of escape, that you may be able to bear it."

This verse informs us that when we reach the valley of adversity, we need to appreciate that:

(i)   No crises will overtake you except such as are common to people;

(ii)   other business climbers have faced this valley, which is common to people;

(iii) God is faithful (Hebrew - Ha'El hanne'eman) and will be faithful to you in this valley;

(iv) God's unwavering commitment to His promises and covenantal relationships. The root word "eman" in Hebrew signifies faithfulness, truth, and certainty;

(v)   You will be given the tools or ability, or knowledge to cross this valley because you will see the way of God's escape;

(vi) You will be able to bear this valley crossing and continue to climb.

In the valley of adversity, the greatest battle will not be defending yourself against malicious forces, but the battle is rather to preserve the sanity of your soul. Good news, the Lord gives us a promise in this Valley: "They will fight against you, But they shall not prevail against you. For I [God] am with you… to deliver you."[79]

Those who are sure that they have God with them (as He is if they are with Him) need not, ought not, to be afraid of whosoever is against them. As you enter this valley and its many channels, set your course to view your adverse circumstances through the eyes of faith, not of sense.

The valley of adversity is not a singular valley but rather a valley with multiple channels, but these are not an exhaustive list of channel valleys, as the enemy of our soul is very subtle in surprising us with new and varied channel valleys.

The Meaning of Adversity

Merriam-Webster online dictionary defines *adversity* as "a state or instance of serious or continued difficulty or misfortune." A more expansive definition was given by Robert Hicks in his book *How a Man Faces Adversity*: [80]

> "*Adversity means life has turned against us. Adversity is a mudslide of bad circumstances. It's an experience of having the forces of life turned against us. This definition then presupposes better times and better fortunes. It's not a 'good news' / 'bad news' joke, and there is no option to hear the good news first. There is no good news, and the bad news, unfortunately, is no joke.*"

Romans 5:3 reminds us that tribulation evokes perseverance and character within us. The word *tribulation* in Greek (*thlipsis*) means "pressure, oppression, affliction, and distress," as well as *trials* or *tribulation.* Unfortunately, in this Valley, you will experience exerting pressure, oppression, affliction, distress, and tribulation.

There are two types of issues that confront us in our daily lives - those we face in the natural world, where we fail exams, encounter business conflicts, or struggle to pay our debts. For the most part, they are under our control and are simply the result of our personal choices. Then there are situations over which we have no control, issues that go from bad to worse like a snowball growing exponentially larger as it rolls downhill. We label the first kind 'problems' while the second falls under the category of 'adversity' or *pathos*. The key here is the control, or lack of it.

I marvel, realizing that though I spent eight years at university and nearly four decades in business life, I somehow missed the course called 'Adversity 101.' Nobody ever breathed a word about it while I was completing a Ph.D. in the faculty of economics and management, nor was I trained by my business mentors on this subject. The sad truth is that the educational system seldom, if ever, prepares the person for adversity.

In the church, we enthusiastically sing "Onward Christian Soldiers." Yet far too often, church members who should be brothers in Christ shoot each other in the back. Then, when we return covered in blood, they ask, "Why are you bleeding? Is there something wrong with you, or have you sinned?" In my own time of trial, I always held out the hope that anyone would walk this valley with me; nobody did but my wife, children, and parents, reminiscent of the parable of the Good Samaritan. But God provided His extraordinary comfort and protection.

The most important lesson when (note I say 'when,' not 'if') walking in the Valley of Adversity: Trust God implicitly.

Trusting God

As someone who graduated from the School of Adversity (for some reason I started to enjoy the School and spent too much time here, overstaying my welcome), I instinctively knew that the assault I was exposed to was different than any other in ways I could not immediately explain. As a youth, and healthy parental guidance, I had learned early on an important lesson - *not to allow myself to become a prisoner of my feelings.*

It's important to note that the only way to prevent being a *prisoner of our feelings* is to live above our feelings and circumstances. This is only possible if we implicitly trust God at all times and declare in our hearts like King David: "I have set the LORD always before me; because He is at my right hand, I shall not be moved."[81] Is God not always with us? Did He not unequivocally promise, "I will never leave you nor forsake you"?[82]

Trusting God is, first and foremost, a matter of the will; it is not dependent on feelings. I have often found myself tempted to feel dejected, moved by difficult circumstances and disappointment, but then I had to consciously pick myself up and choose to trust my Heavenly Father. When I choose to trust God, my feelings of trust eventually follow, but it's always in that order - *feelings always follow choices.* Making the right choices generates positive feelings that motivate us to continue to trust, hope, and work hard. Making wrong choices gives rise to negative feelings, which lead to disappointment, discouragement, and possibly depression.

Trusting God implicitly isn't always as easy as it sounds. Nevertheless, He is completely trustworthy. Whether it feels like it or not, God always knows best. In fact, what we see might make us wonder or doubt, but Scripture tells us that "[God's] thoughts are not your thoughts, nor are your ways [God's] ways."[83] At that juncture, we must choose whether to believe what God says about Himself in His Word or what He has revealed to us, or fall prey to our feelings and circumstances.

Attending the School of Adversity, the choice for me was easy, though waiting for my feelings to follow came much slower. Regrettably, in my youth, I never had much interest in dogs until one day, a veterinarian said to me in passing, "Get yourself a dog. They are so forgiving." I took her advice literally and bought a Labrador for each of my three children. She was right; dogs are

144

remarkably forgiving and have also taught me not only about love but also revealed more about my favorite and beloved subject of 'grace' (I used to buy stickers with the word 'grace' and stuck them daily on my chest as a constant reminder for me).

In 2 Chronicles 20, we read how the Mites and Kites (my nicknames) declared war against Israel. Several men came and told King Jehoshaphat, "A great multitude is coming against you from beyond the sea, from Syria, and they are in Hazazon Tamar."[84] Upon hearing this, King Jehoshaphat's first reaction was to *seek the LORD*.

When in adversity or under attack, the scriptural law of *first reaction* is key - the very key to our success. We must honor God the way Jehoshaphat did by turning to Him FIRST. Be careful to turn to God first, and not simply as a last resort, because the law of first reaction is the key that will unlock a miracle, even for those who are forever suspicious of miracles. King Jehoshaphat made this incredible statement:

> *"O LORD God of our fathers, are You not God in heaven, and do You not rule over all the kingdoms of the nations, and in Your hand is there not power and might, so that no one is able to withstand You? Are You, not our God, who drove out the inhabitants of this land before Your people, Israel, and gave it to the descendants of Abraham, Your friend forever?"*[85]

It is no easy feat to trust God during an attack, but to please God, we must respond out of faith. Scripture says: "Without faith, it is impossible to please Him, for he who comes to God must believe that He is and that He is a rewarder of those who diligently seek Him."[86] The alternative to faith is choosing to be sucked under and held captive by feelings of fear, anxiety, or grief, with no options and no way out of the situation.

John Newton, author of my favorite hymn, *Amazing Grace*, is a fine example of faith under fire when he watched cancer slowly and painfully drain the life of his wife. In recounting those days, Newton said:

> *"Through the whole of my painful trial, I attended all my stated and occasional services, as usual, and a stranger would scarcely have discovered, either by my words or looks, that I was in trouble. [The long adversity] did not prevent me from preaching a single sermon, and I preached on the day of her death… I likewise preached three times while she lay dead in the house…. And after she was deposited in the vault, I preached her funeral sermon."*[87]

Newton applied the law of first reaction, thus saving himself an inordinate amount of grief and distraction. He chose to trust God, immediately turning to Him in an attitude of complete dependence. I wholeheartedly agree with the revelatory observation given by best-selling author Jerry Bridges:

"Whenever I teach on the subject of personal holiness, I always stress that we are responsible for obeying the will of God, but that we are dependent upon the Holy Spirit for the enabling power to do it. The same principle applies in the realm of trusting God. We are responsible to trust Him in times of adversity, but we are dependent upon the Holy Spirit to enable us to do so."[88]

We trust God in this Valley because we come to understand that only in this Valley does God prune His vine.

God Works through Adversity

In the words of Jesus, God is the Gardener[89] who prunes the branches of His vineyard. The healthy vine requires both nourishment and pruning. Through the Word of God, we are nourished,[90] but it is only through adversity that we are pruned.

God intends that we grow through the disciplines of adversity as well as through instruction from His Word. The psalmist forever links adversity to instruction in God's training process when he says, "Blessed is the man you discipline, O Lord, the man you teach from your law."[91]

It is imperative to grasp that God cannot fail in His purpose for adversity in our lives, as Philippians 1:6 illustrates: "Being confident of this very thing, that He who has begun a good work in you will complete it until the day of Jesus Christ." In this regard, Horatius Bonar, a 19th-century Scottish pastor,[92] wrote:

"He who is carrying it on is not one who can be baffled and forced to give up His design. He is able to carry it out in the unlikeliest circumstances and against the most resolute resistance. Everything must give way before Him. This thought is, I confess, one of the most comforting connected with discipline if it could fail! If God could be frustrated in His designs after we have suffered so much, it would be awful."

By now, you might be wondering why I'm citing so much Scripture. Trust me – you are going to need it deeply as you navigate these painfully challenging valleys. The first channel valley this stream takes us into is the Channel Valley of Confinement - a prison of circumstances.

Channel Valley of Confinement

Bible teacher F.B. Meyer once observed, "Whenever you get into a prison of circumstances, be on watch. Prisons are rare places for seeing things. It was in prison that Bunyan saw his wondrous allegory. Paul met the Lord. John looked through heaven's open door, and Joseph saw God's mercy. God has no chance to show His mercy to some of us except when we are in some distressing sorrow. The night is the time to see the stars."[93]

The Valley of Confinement performs some painful surgery on our character. The purpose of this surgery is not to destroy us but to give us a new perspective to prepare us for His purposes.[94] After the surgery, we will be fundamentally changed in who we are and what we will be, ready to submit to God's leading.

The Apostle Paul was literally imprisoned, and not once did he say that he was a "Roman prisoner," but described his circumstances in three revealing ways:

"I, Paul, the prisoner of Christ Jesus"[95] - *"the prisoner of the Lord"*[96] – *"I am an ambassador in chains."*[97]

Paul clearly understood that even though the Romans had arrested him, it was God who had planned his imprisonment, and as such, he insisted that he was God's prisoner. Only one type of surgery occurs in this Valley - heart surgery. If the heart is arrogant and uncircumcised, then we are on our way to destruction. Circumcision of the heart is necessary because "the heart is deceitful above all things and desperately wicked."[98]

Physically, an uncircumcised heart contains a whole host of toxic, unsavory things under its foreskin. Pastor Dr. Olukoya says, "These materials have proved to be capable of causing cancer. An uncircumcised man could perform all the functions of the circumcised, but yet an uncircumcised man is a disaster, a time bomb waiting for the time of explosion. Likewise, an uncircumcised heart is a walking corpse."[99]

Unfortunately, circumcision is a painful procedure. The uncircumcised experience pain when their issues are addressed. That's why it takes prison to force us to deal with our issues and become more intimate with God. While our enemies try to take advantage of us when they see us walking in this Valley, they foolishly believe they have the upper hand. They are merely pawns in the hands of God to force us to examine our hearts and humble ourselves before Him.

The Channel Valley of Confinement flows into the Channel Valley of Trauma.

Channel Valley of Trauma

The *Merriam-Webster Online Dictionary* defines trauma as "a disordered psychic or behavioral state resulting from severe mental or emotional stress or physical injury." It is, by nature, distressing and completely overwhelming, consuming us in a fog of confusion.

In a traumatic situation, something is happening that is completely out of our control, and it feels big enough to wreck even the most stellar career. In fact, an essential ingredient in trauma is the reality of the threat to our well-being and our sanity. Freud recognized this when he said that in trauma, a person feels completely helpless and ineffective in the face of what is perceived to be overwhelming danger.[100]

Jasmin Cori, who spent her childhood in a traumatized state, said that trauma "happens when a parent gets drunk and beats a child. It happens when a caretaker or sibling crosses boundaries, messing with your mind and betraying your trust. It happens in all kinds of ways and under all kinds of cover. Even in the name of love."[101]

The body reacts to a traumatic event as an emergency, with either a fight-or-flight response or freezing, much like a deer freezes before the headlights of a car. This event is also called the immobility response because we become immobilized, paralyzed by our terror.[102] Whilst walking in this Valley, I wanted to punch the perpetrators until my mother wisely encouraged me to freeze my fists.

One of the innovative researchers in trauma, Peter A. Levine, believes that trauma results when our instinctual responses to a traumatic event aren't allowed to cycle all the steps to the point of resolution. When an emergency occurs, we freeze (or our mother advises us to freeze our fists), and we are unable to shake it off. Without a way to safely release the pent-up energy in the nervous system, that sense of being on alert stays in the system and could result in symptoms of post-traumatic stress disorder. Under the pressure of such un-discharged energy, the system becomes more sensitized, and the next trauma (and there are many moments of trauma when exposed to Chieftans) or other emergencies only compounds the problem. As things pile up, each new trauma adds more energy, and symptoms get worse; as a result, we feel more and more helpless when something difficult happens because we haven't learned how to deal with it physiologically.[103]

Following a traumatic event or repeated trauma, people react in different ways, experiencing a wide range of physical and emotional reactions. There is no 'right' or 'wrong' way to think or feel when confronted by abnormal events. According to the Sidran Institute,[104] the emotional and psychological symptoms of trauma include:

o   substance dependence and abuse,

o   personality disorders (especially borderline personality disorder),

o   depression,

o   anxiety (including post-traumatic stress disorder),

o   dissociative disorders, and

o   eating disorders, to name a few.

The feelings described above will be felt whilst traversing this Valley, but the symptoms change radically from day to day, i.e., from one day feeling anger to feeling disconnected or struggling to concentrate the next day.

According to *Psychology Today*,[105] psychological trauma may set in after a distressing or life-threatening event and may result in extreme anxiety or post-traumatic stress disorder, or victims may have ongoing relationship problems and unresolved self-esteem issues.

In most legal jurisdictions, a defendant can be charged in court with a criminal act if the defendant inflicted an injury on another that resulted in a traumatic condition. To prove that the defendant is guilty of this crime, it must ordinarily be shown that the defendant willfully and unlawfully inflicted the injury, which resulted in a traumatic condition.[106] Inflicting trauma on others is not a simple misdemeanor; it is a serious criminal act with serious consequences.

The Valley of Trauma leads straight to the Channel Valley of Brokenness.

Channel Valley of Brokenness

Brokenness is all part of God's perfect plan: *the way up with God is the way down.* Read Philippians 2 in order to grasp this truthfully.

In his book, *The Blessings of Brokenness,* prolific Christian author Charles Stanley describes brokenness this way: "to be shattered, to feel as if our entire world has fallen apart, or perhaps been blown apart… Brokenness is often accompanied by emptiness – a void that cannot be filled, a sorrow that cannot be comforted, a wound for which there is no balm."[107]

When Moses was called by God to be His champion to lead the Israelites out of Egypt, Moses, in effect, replied: "I am not capable of this mammoth task, God."[108] This is exactly where God wants us to be. We simply cannot do it in our own strength, but as we place our faith in Him, God does it on our behalf. We simply need to be the willing vessel. God alone can empower us with the provision and the power to accomplish what He calls us to do. He imparts His power through us by His Spirit to accomplish His humanly impossible objectives.

Brokenness also brings us to the place where we realize with great awareness what the Apostle Paul wrote to the Ephesians: "For we do not wrestle against flesh and blood, but against principalities, against powers, against the rulers of the darkness of this age, against spiritual hosts of wickedness in the heavenly places."[109]

Bringing about Kingdom change in the marketplace, raising a Christian family, or preaching the gospel must be done by the power of the Holy Spirit to the glory of God if it is to be of any eternal value at all. Such submission to the work of the Spirit is often motivated by a season of brokenness, which is why I often experienced the Christian life as one of paradox, as I said: the way up with God is the way down.[110]

In the Valley of Brokenness, true power lies: "Not by might, nor by power, but by [His] Spirit."[111] We never get to the position of power where our faith is no longer challenged. Rather, "we are called again and again to a position of total surrender, total trust, total yielding, total commitment."[112]

The Valley of Brokenness and the next Valley of Humiliation actually run parallel to each other.

Channel Valley of Humiliation

In John Bunyan's memorable novel "The Pilgrim's Progress," the Valley of Humiliation is best described to us. This Valley is a symbolic place (but also very real) where the leading character, 'Christian,' encounters the dangers of 'pride and forgetfulness.' It is a place where a Christian is brought to an acute awareness of his sinfulness and unworthiness before God, but also where he learns to find solitude in God's grace.

'Humiliation' can be defined as the action of humiliating someone or the state of being humiliated. Few, if any, authors can describe this Valley better than John Bunyan (who was confined to many years in prison), so best we consider what he has to say in this regard:

"Now they began to go down the hill into the Valley of Humiliation. It was a steep hill, and the way was slippery, but they were very careful, so they got down pretty well. When they were down in the valley, Piety said to Christiana, This is the place where Christian, your husband, met with the foul fiend Apollyon and where they had that dreadful fight that they had: I know you cannot but have heard thereof. But be of good courage; as long as you have here Mr. Great-Heart to be your guide and conductor, we hope you will fare the better. So when these two had committed the pilgrims unto the conduct of their guide, he went forward, and they went after.

Mr. Great-Heart: Then said Mr. Great-Heart, We need not be so afraid of this valley, for here is nothing to hurt us unless we procure it to ourselves. It is true, Christian did here meet with Apollyon, with whom he had also sore combat, but that fray was the fruit of those slips that he got in his going down the hill: for they that get slips there must look for combats here. And hence it is that this valley has got such a hard name. For the common people, when they hear that some frightful thing has befallen such a one in such a place, are of the opinion that that place is haunted with some foul fiend or evil spirit; when, alas! It is for the fruit of their doing that such things do befall them there. This Valley of Humiliation is of itself as fruitful a place as any the crow flies over, and I am persuaded, if we could hit upon it, we might find somewhere hereabouts something that might give us an account of why Christian was so hardly beset in this place."

Through the mouth of Bunyan's character, Mr. Greatheart, who says: "It is those who 'slip' coming down into the valley [of humiliation], who must expect conflicts here… This valley, in itself, is a peaceful, fruitful country. But pilgrims, not knowing how to adjust themselves to humiliation, yield to wrong feelings. Then Satan, taking advantage of their moods, sends his imps… and they attack these immature disciples… many humble people have made their homes here and live in contentment… it is those who

156

have accustomed themselves to living at higher altitudes who have the most trouble here."

If the Valley of Humiliation isn't daunting enough, the menacing antagonists from the 'Valley Hunters' go out of their way to track you down.

The Valley Hunters

Be alert: these Valley Hunters are a major headache and a serious source of trouble for you. Who are they? Never heard of these hunters? They are individuals whose sole mission is to hunt down pilgrims in the valley. Experienced to spot the vulnerable, they chip away at your financial and emotional resources, fully aware that your judgment is clouded during times of hardship.

Since adversity often brings intense emotions, these can overwhelm the rational part of the brain, making it harder to think intelligently, weigh options, or make objective decisions. Hardship also wears down mental and emotional energy, thereby diluting your decision-making ability.

In my experience, the Valley Hunters do not operate as a unified group - they typically act alone, like the tentacles of an octopus, each one draining you bit by bit. I will do my best to explain, drawing also from others who have done groundwork in this area.

In their research, *Personality Disorders in Modern Life*, Millon and Davis[113] define personality as "a complex pattern of deeply embedded psychological characteristics that are expressed automatically in almost every area of psychological functioning."

Our temperament is the "biological-genetic template that interacts with our environment,"[114] whereas our character is "largely the outcome of the process of socialization, the acts and imprints of our environment and nurture on our psyche during the formative years (0-6 and in adolescence)."[115] Our character is the set of all the acquired traits we possess, often shaped by our cultural-social environment.

Personality disorders are dysfunctions affecting our whole identity, both in temperament and character; they are tears or rips in the fabric of who we are. Someone is considered mentally ill if, according to Sam Vaknin, the person's "behavior causes him or others discomfort, and is dysfunctional, self-defeating, and self-destructive even by his own yardsticks."

This now gives a better picture of what a Valley Hunter is like: "dysfunctional, self-defeating, and self-destructive even by his own yardsticks." They are also incapable of empathy or a normal conscience. This deep dysfunction entangles you in its web of traits and drains you, so a Valley Hunter is difficult to discern at the outset. As I have said previously, hardship wears you down mentally and emotionally, thereby diluting your decision-making ability, i.e., your ability to discern friend from foe.

If you are fortunate enough to recognize that a new acquaintance might be a Valley Hunter, what steps should you take next? Promptly withdraw! That's because you lack the skill or the energy to handle the dysfunctional behavior of a Valley Hunter. If you ignore my warning and choose to associate with the individual, it will likely prolong your time in the Valley of Adversity by months or even years.

How can you steer clear of Valley Hunters during your season of adversity? It's unlikely you will completely avoid encountering them, much like the chances of escaping a bout of the flu in any given season. I am obviously not a psychologist, and do not wish to venture into the character qualities I found prevalent among the Valley Hunters I encountered, but one telltale sign is that when communicating in person with them they occasionally slip into a daze-like coma (I'm not sure who they are attempting to reach, but it's not an Angel).

What do Valley Hunters hope to achieve from their mission? They don't ask this question because their actions are dysfunctional. By now, you might be curious to learn more, but I intentionally choose not to elaborate further - these distractions don't deserve more attention. You are destined for heaven, not the furnace.

Now that we have considered the emotions and experiences of the various Channel Valleys, what's it like to take a dip beneath the surface?

Looking Beneath the Surface

Whilst minding our own business in the Valley, we occasionally take a dip in the pool, where I experienced God revealing annoying creaks to show in the floor of our lives - circumstances or people that are a constant annoyance to us. These irritations are God's way of drawing our attention to toxic blind spots. Through them, we are forced to do some serious self-examination.

The history of our family business, which exceeded its centenary, is quite humbling in the sense that the business has experienced such wonderful success over ten decades. I had personally witnessed God's gracious miracles on an incredible scale, yet there was a toxic blind spot. In fact, it was only when we entered our season of adversity that we realized the nature of that blind spot.

Let me explain our blind spot, and most likely yours, too. First of all, I always believed that the term 'collaboration' was written with a small 'c' as in 'considerate,' but I learned the hard way that in many cases it should be written in Capitals with a 'C' as in 'Chilling' (i.e., Chilling Experiences). Also, I used to confuse too many 'partners' with 'friends.' My brothers and I were brought up in a committed Christian home, as were my parents and grandparents (I am not sure how far down the line it goes). We believed, probably like you, that all people have the same good intentions toward us that we have toward them. Actually, this belief system is a fatal mistake, as Scripture warns us for good reason that "I [Jesus] send you out as sheep in the midst of wolves. Therefore, be wise as serpents and harmless as doves."[116]

Recognize that not everyone in business operates with good intentions. While some individuals are sincere, others may have hidden motives, pursue personal gain, or misinterpret your words. This makes it essential to distinguish between what can be shared innocently with friends and family and what should be communicated more carefully to strangers or professional contacts. Family and true friends typically understand your tone, context, and intent, but strangers do not. Oversharing personal or sensitive information can backfire, either through deliberate misuse or unintended disclosure. That's why discretion, clear boundaries, and situational awareness are vital in business interactions.

My father only had one piece of advice for me when I got married, which was to make sure that my "wife was always right under all circumstances." That is not a crack in wisdom because I have experienced the sage advice with great success (happily married for thirty years). Business relationships would be more successful if there were healthy reciprocity between the partners, with each partner continually showing deference toward the other.

I read about a significant conflict that once occurred between two equal shareholding business partners. As a result, one partner left with the intention of ending the relationship, while the other partner left a sincere note on his partner's desk saying, "I hereby gift 5% of my shares in the business to you, making you the majority partner, please share how I can better help you, Boss?" The prideful partner instantly realized that his friend was the bigger man, and the tables were immediately turned, so he gave up his domineering position in the company and handed the reins of the business over to his meeker friend. It takes far more than mere capital to manage well in business; it also requires the gracious and considerate character traits to truly succeed.

Mark Twain gives us important advice on how to deal with unhealthy associations: "Keep away from people who belittle your ambitions. Small people always do that, but the really great make you feel that you, too, can become great." The sad truth is that good partners are the only ones who will make you feel great, so don't expect any encouragement from those who belittle you. I had a difficult time when I tried to Google the meaning of the phrase "good business partners." Most of the articles dealt with "how to find a good partner." To this day, I still have not found an appropriate definition of a "good business partner," so I wish to offer some thoughts of my own.

To seek a good business partner, it is imperative that you *start with yourself.* 'You' must be that good partner before seeking high values in others, because we are all equal at the foot of the cross. To be a good partner, Philippians 2:3 says it best: "Let nothing be done through selfish ambition or conceit, but in lowliness of mind let each esteem others better than himself." A good partner is simply one who shares and lives out these values while applying gracious acts and understands the power of reciprocity.

The environment in which deceivers are nurtured is one of selfish ambition and conceit; the principle of partnership does not even enter their framework of thinking. If you, like me, tend to confuse your 'friendly Monster' with a 'caring partner,' you are on a collision course with a stunning wake-up call. The good news is that we always stand a chance of success if we take heed. Forewarned is forearmed; once we know the difference between a Monster and a partner, we strategize accordingly.

My search for a "good business partner" ultimately led me to the mirror - there he was. I realized that by stepping up, leading with integrity, and acting with purpose, I could become the kind of partner I was hoping to find - and, in doing so, attract the right counterpart.

There are others walking in the same Valley; you are not alone. You will see a lot of dust swept up by so many looking for a tall tree to climb (not easy to find a tree in the desert), away from the reality of the Valley. Clean the dust from your eyes and find that individual who can walk this road with you, or at the very least be a friend to a fellow traveler.

Walking with Others

A story is told of a man who, having been lost in a dense forest for days, finally sat down on a log and wept uncontrollably. As he cried, he heard someone coming through the bush and leapt up and wrapped his arms around his newfound friend. He uttered, "Thank goodness, I'm saved! Now we can get out of here." Wiping a tear from his own eye, the other man replied, "I'm lost too, but I'll walk with you."

When walking the valley of adversity, sadly, most of the friends and colleagues you believed were your allies will desert you, so expect this and prepare yourself for it. It may be helpful to reflect upon the six categories of people who influenced my life and I believe will shape your life:

- o 'Category Fence' are those who enjoy sitting on the fence and hurling stones;

- o 'Category False' are those who falsely accuse you and/or passively watch as you are being stoned;

- o 'Category Misuse' are those who do not readily judge but do misuse you for personal benefit;

- o 'Category Reject' are those who reject you and/or never appreciate anything you do for them;

- 'Category Respect' do not like you but nevertheless respect you and/or those who like you and positively influence your life;

- 'Category Love' they love you unconditionally.

Those in categories one and two are the most dangerous. People in categories three and four are harmless, but have good boundaries around them. Those in category five will positively influence your life, and you should befriend them.

Ah, now prepare for this Gem. Read this paragraph carefully, because it is often believed that the category six individual can only be your parents, wife, and children. In a season of adversity, God adds to your quiver a much greater complement of category six type individuals; it is God's hidden blessing to you.

While minding your own business in the Valley and witnessing others run for cover, there is always the niggling question of whether there is a possible way out?

Is There Another Way?

We may never know for certain, but in fact, adversity is probably the most effective way for God to get our undivided attention. Is there another way? The question is the wrong one to ask, because …

A surprise awaits you as you traverse the various valleys, one I certainly discovered, that adversity is a springboard into far greater things, and today I can truly call the Valley of Adversity my dear Friend.

How often have you heard a sermon or testimony that stirred your spirit and sparked a desire to live by a higher standard? Yet repeatedly, some earthly concerns flooded your mind and washed away all your noble intentions mere moments after you exited the church door.

Most often, it takes more than a sermon to get our attention. Not even heartfelt conviction is enough to bring about permanent transformation. Usually, it takes a jolt of some kind to get our attention to make changes to our lives. In his excellent book, *The Problem of Pain,* C. S. Lewis put it this way:

> *"God whispers to us in our pleasures, speaks to our conscience, but shouts in our pains: it is His megaphone to rouse a deaf world."*[117]

When all is well in our lives, we easily forget God and drift into a world of apathetic self-reliance. To make matters worse, we begin to confuse our sense of well-being with advanced spirituality. But return to that same individual following adversity, and you'll find that what at one time was of great importance holds no more attraction, and that which was of little concern has now become the only concern. Suddenly, God has the individual's complete attention.

Hot Chocolate Time

Whilst in a season of adversity, many strange happenings occur, which I refer to as the 'hot chocolate time.' When adversity strikes, one's life goes in another direction. My pre-adversity season was marked by hard work, with no lunch or coffee breaks, a lot of television, much traveling, little reading or writing (except for the times when I was completing my degrees), and little time for friends. During my adversity season, I dropped television, read extensively, prayed consistently, thought more about others, and ordered lots of hot chocolate.

When the great prophet Elijah walked the Valley of Adversity, he was encouraged to stand upon a mountain and hear from the Lord. And then:

> *"...the Lord passed by, and a great and strong wind tore into the mountains and broke the rocks in pieces before the Lord, but the Lord was not in the wind, and after the wind an earthquake, but the Lord was not in the earthquake, and after the earthquake a fire, but the Lord was not in the fire, and after the fire a still small voice."*[118]

Elijah instinctively knew that the Lord's voice was not in the commotion but in "a still small voice." It is the small things that will sustain and nurture you during your adversity season. More surprisingly, the 'hot chocolate time' is when God lovingly communicates to you through the actions of strangers.

Herein lies the secret: *God communicates differently, always in a still, small voice, but you need to know how to recognize the blessings that come your way.* Therefore, my 'hot chocolate time' is the soul reaching out to God as a dealer in hope and trust. You are consciously aware that God will be your Provider and will fight the enemy on your behalf. Instead of panicking, you remain calm; instead of first putting on your battle helmet, you first pray; instead of considering negative news, you count your many blessings from other sources, and instead of running blindly onto the battlefield, you order hot chocolate (whilst remaining watchful and prepared) in complete trust in a faithful God.

This time is a sign that Philippians 4:6 has taken on new meaning in your life: "Be anxious for nothing, but in everything by prayer and supplication, with thanksgiving, let your requests be made known to God." This call to be rid of anxiety is a call to let nothing unsettle your heart. That's why, when all hell breaks loose, you can place an order for a hot chocolate in complete stillness. This supernatural peace is not being ignorant of what is happening around you or doing nothing about your circumstances; it merely implies a heart at peace.

My brother even cautioned me, "Some are under the impression that you have lost it, Alan." Others called me a "man out of touch with reality," and my adversaries were licking their lips with the feast that was before them. "I hear you," I said, "but can you get me another 'hot chocolate' please?" [After more flaming outbursts from my friends, I had to collect the hot chocolate myself].

What everyone failed to recognize is that I had experienced a rebirth from a man with small faith to a warrior with large faith. I started to communicate wisely with my many adversaries with restored confidence and deep insights. When adversity strikes, and the enemy rages against you, relish those hot chocolate times and collect the drink yourself (if required).

Hold on — just when you feel you have arrived, let go of your hot drink and glance slightly to the right at the rising of the sun. There is still a strange-looking area, which I don't know how to exactly describe, but the best explanation I could find is that of an 'alluvial fan.' This raving fan awaits you.

The Alluvial Fan

In geography terms, an 'alluvial fan' is described by one commentator as "nature's inland estuary - where torrents from bone-dry canyons spill wide across the valley floor, spreading life and silt with every rare storm."

In spiritual terms, as it relates to adversity, the 'alluvial fan' is my own practical explanation of the Scriptural term 'regeneration.' It's best to turn to the renowned Charles Spurgeon to shed light on the mysteries of faith that are captured in the concept of 'regeneration':

"We need not wonder that there are some mysteries in our holy faith, for there are mysteries everywhere. In nature, there are ten thousand things that we cannot understand. In our own bodies, there are inexplicable mysteries. He who thinks for only a little while, even of so simple a matter as to how it is that food is gradually turned into flesh, knowing how impossible it would be for us to do it by any chemical process or mechanical apparatus, will see that there is a mystery in every human life, a secret chamber into which the eyes of man cannot look." [119]

Regeneration, as it applies to the Christian faith, is one of the 'mysteries of faith.' Regeneration is the spiritual rebirth or renewal of an individual through the work of the Holy Spirit. It is the divine process by which a person, once spiritually dead, is brought to new life in Christ. It is entirely the work of the Holy Spirit; the works of man have no part in it – hence it is a mystery.

The clearest mention of the term "regeneration," directly linking it to salvation and the renewing work of the Holy Spirit, is given in Titus 3:5 –

"not by works of righteousness which we have done, but according to His mercy He saved us, through the washing of regeneration and renewing of the Holy Spirit."

The alluvial fan in the valley of adversity, in terms of this Chapter, is also the regeneration that takes place in terms of

Romans 12:2 in the "renewing of your mind, that you may prove what is that good and acceptable and perfect will of God."

People may hear the Gospel with their ears, but they cannot truly grasp its meaning until the Spirit of God opens their minds and hearts. An unregenerated mind is as incapable of understanding the Gospel as a horse is of grasping economics - it lies completely beyond the reach of the natural, worldly mind.

Regeneration also occurs in the heart as expounded in Ezekiel 36:26 – "I will give you a new heart and put a new spirit within you; I will take the heart of stone out of your flesh and give you a heart of flesh." God promises to replace a hardened, unresponsive heart with one that is tender and alive to His will. It's about a fundamental inner transformation.

As you journey through the valley of adversity, the Holy Spirit is actively shaping the renewal of your mind and heart. This transformation is continuous - unfolding moment by moment - and is focused on deepening your knowledge and love of God and gaining greater clarity about your divine purpose.

In the context of my narrative, the difference between the channel valleys and the alluvial fan is this: the valleys represent experiences you walk through consciously and tangibly, while the alluvial fan symbolizes the quiet, unseen transformation of your mind and heart. This inner change unfolds without your awareness until you look back and realize that God was guiding, protecting, and shaping you all along, extending a precious gift through the transformative mind and heart work of the Holy Spirit.

So, in summary, as many dangerous channel valleys are confronted, we deem ourselves forgotten, but out of nowhere and suddenly, we receive this striking manifestation that Jehovah-Nissi ("Jehovah is our banner") has provided divine protection, as in a banner that guides and defends. Before us, as our eyes have become accustomed to the darkness of our situation, we witness in the distance a mass of calm water, which we now realize is the dark and dry channel valleys that have led us to the sea of magnificent grace.

Still, a pronounced break is required from you. Don't run too hastily to this sea because after a remarkable deliverance, when your trials have paused, when new joys begin to bloom, and after a time of deep discouragement, your spirit can once more rise and bask in God's light. Then, once again, before proceeding to the sea of magnificent grace, you should first return to the foot of Christ's cross, and there, by His shed blood, renew your dedication to the Lord.

The Sea of Magnificent Grace

The heartwarming true story is told of the late Bishop of Jerusalem, who, when involved as a missionary in Abyssinia, once found himself in a season of deep spiritual depression, then retired and ran into a literal cavern. There, he poured out his heart in earnest supplication, pleading that God would not leave him but be beside him during this painful trial. He remained in the cavern for a long time. When he found strength and rose from his slumber, his eyes had become accustomed to the darkness, and he saw that he had been there with a hyena and her cubs, which had miraculously not been permitted to attack him.

This, too, was the experience of the nation of Judah, which could not see that God was for them; all they could see was that Assyria was against them. It was during this period, when the nation was under terrible fear and dread of the Assyrians, that the prophet Isaiah penned these words from the Lord: "For thus says the Lord GOD, the Holy One of Israel: 'In returning and rest you shall be saved; In quietness and confidence shall be your strength.'"[120]

These are powerful words of encouragement, and by taking the verse apart, we learn the following:

- o "In returning," the Lord is calling them to return from pursuing other solutions. He is encouraging them to return their focus on Him alone as their sole source of provision.
- o "And rest" – in calling them to rest, God was encouraging them to be still and relax and stop all frenetic activity. God was saying that He was preparing to act on their behalf.
- o "In quietness" – the word is the same word used in Scripture to describe wine that "settles" on its lees.[121] As wine is being prepared, there is a process whereby it is

placed on a shelf in total stillness so that the tiny particles of sediment can settle to the bottom. So, God is literally saying to them, "Settle down, please."

- o "And confidence" – this word corresponds thematically with "returning," and it's as though the Lord were saying, "You need to recover the certainty that I will take care of you. Unbelief and fear have robbed you of your confidence, and it's time to return and renew your stand of faith in who I am and in what I have promised you in My Word."[122]

If God has graciously crowned you with His love and tender mercies, then make sure that He reigns anew on the throne of your mind and heart. Since we rely on the fulfillment of new promises from God, let us also offer fresh commitments to Him and renew our prayers so that the promises we've already made are not forgotten or neglected. Since our minds and hearts have been made new, our prayers have changed – we no longer plead, 'Get me out of this.' Instead, we come before God to reaffirm our commitment, and our new prayer becomes, "renew a right spirit within me."

Our journey through this marketplace has led us down many rugged paths, resembling a vast, howling wilderness - like the Sahara itself. Emotionally barren, it has drained us, surrounded by scorching sands and echoing with the stories of those who lost their way in this merciless expanse. Yet, amid the heat and desolation, something extraordinary emerged - rising suddenly from the dust,

I witnessed that a renowned plant took root. As it grew, it blossomed. The bud unfurled into the regal Protea, and beside it, unexpectedly, bloomed a striking red rose. Please note that the flowers referenced here hold personal significance in my life (you will witness different flowers) - they carry a coded message meant for me (your flowers will carry a personalized coded message for you), which I discuss in more detail later in this book.

These majestic plants had been planted in the desolate wilderness by a Divine Hand, gently silencing my doubts and disbelief. And then, as if the miracle of their blossoming were not wonder enough, I saw that God had guided me to the shores of the Sea of Magnificent Grace.

CHAPTER 7
THE GRACE FACTOR

"For the law was given through Moses, but grace and truth came through Jesus Christ."

(John 1:17)

A Symphony of Grace

Since the beginning of time, there has been no shortage of visionaries, mystics, and cranks who have conjured up brave new worlds that have encouraged hope and exhibited folly in equal measure. Arthur Waugh, a prolific English journalist of the 1950's agrees that "the human mind is inspired enough when it comes to inventing horrors; it is when it tries to invent a Heaven that it shows itself cloddish."

The marketplace has undoubtedly deteriorated; it is now in the last stages of decay. This Chapter is not intended to propose a brave new utopia of commerce, but rather to introduce a rare ingredient to the marketplace which will help to transform the prevailing downward trend.

Let's turn our attention to possibly the most poignant passage of the Bible found in 1 Corinthians 13: "Though I speak with the tongues of men and of angels, but have not love, I have become sounding brass or a clanging cymbal. And though I have the gift of prophecy, and understand all mysteries and all knowledge, and though I have all faith, so that I could remove mountains, but have not love, I am nothing. And though I bestow all my goods to feed the poor, and though I give my body to be burned, but have not love, it profits me nothing."

This verse sounds much like a symphony of grace. It expresses tenderness and warmth that reflects the heart of God. And if that's the case, how can we do less than love others, when God has such incredible love for us, who are unlovable?

While commerce now faces a debt dilemma fuelled by inherent distrust, it has nevertheless always been bankrupt, regarding the more pressing issue of 'grace.' The sad truth is that people in the marketplace can be excused for the lack of cash at their disposal, but they cannot be exempt from a lack of grace. The world and the marketplace long for grace.

The Meaning of Grace

What I mean by 'grace' in this book is the embodiment of 1 Corinthians 13:13 – "And now abide [meaning it's eternal] faith, hope, love, these three; but the greatest of these is love." Amplified means: faith in God, hope in God, love to God, and love to neighbour.

A word of Knowledge – 'grace dispels coded arrows.' In picture format, grace represents the entire Universe, whereas marketplace codes represent a dust particle in comparison.

The word 'grace' can have a variety of other meanings. In the *Oxford English Dictionary,* the noun of grace refers to "smoothness and elegance of movement," whereas the verb refers to "bringing honor or credit to (someone or something) by one's attendance or participation."

Strong's Concordance defines grace as "the state of kindness and favor toward someone, often with a focus on a benefit given to the object." *The Oxford English Dictionary* goes further to describe it as "courteous goodwill."

In the context of this book, the term 'grace' goes on to include the qualities of kindness and mercy, expecting nothing in return, but even more importantly, *freely given.* Grace uses both feelings and actions to express itself, and always involves an element of self-sacrifice.

Let's try to consider a complicated understanding of the term 'grace' by means of a simplified allegory. Assume you were stopped by a policeman for a speeding violation. If the policeman gives you a speeding ticket, then that's *justice*. If, on the other hand, the policeman decides to let you off the hook, that's *mercy*. However, if the policeman gives you both a speeding ticket and a ticket for your worn tires, then that's *severe justice*. But if the policeman lets you off the hook and takes the trouble to briefly teach you how to be a better driver, that's *grace*.

Commerce today is so void of grace that when it appears, it automatically raises suspicion – a rather dismal situation. In that regard, if we study the outstanding Victor Hugo novel, *Les Miserables*, we see 19th-century Frenchman Jean Valjean being relentlessly hunted for decades by the ruthless Inspector Javert. But even under unceasing pressure, Valjean's actions, whether in business or his personal life, are something akin to grace. Conversely, the evil Javert perfectly portrays what it's like to be pursued by a graceless individual.

Why the Significance of Grace?

The fact that grace dispels harmful codes is a good enough reason for the significance of grace. But there is another reason, because it's God's ordained way to business sanity and success. A bible example to illustrate my point:

179

In 2 Kings 5, we read of the healing of the mighty warrior Naaman. The King of Aram had great admiration for his warrior, because he had achieved great victories for the King, but he suffered from leprosy. A young girl encourages Namaan to go visit the prophet of God for his healing, and when he asked permission from the King to visit the prophet, the King sent a letter of introduction on behalf of Namaan to Elisha the prophet to heal his faithful warrior.

Then Naaman went with his horses and chariot, and he stood at the door of Elisha's house. And Elisha sent a messenger to him, saying, "Go and wash in the Jordan seven times, and your flesh shall be restored to you, and you shall be clean."

But Naaman became angry and walked away. "I thought he would certainly come out to meet me!" he said. "I expected him to wave his hand over the leprosy and call on the name of the Lord his God and heal me! Aren't the rivers of Damascus, the Abana and the Pharpar, better than any of the rivers of Israel? Why shouldn't I wash in them and be healed?" So Naaman turned and went away in a prideful rage.

However, Namaan's officers reasoned with him to listen to the prophet. After some persuasion, Naaman went down to the Jordan River and dipped himself seven times, as the man of God had instructed him. And his skin became as healthy as the skin of a young child, and he was healed!

God's ways are not our ways. What may seem a simple solution to you is God's way of escape for you from the shackles of business misery – now go wash yourself in the River of Grace and do it several times, just as Namaan was instructed.

There are three principles that can be taken from the concept of grace: kindness, goodwill, and favor.

The Golden Rule

The Golden Rule is a rare gem, standing the test of time, as captured by Jesus' words in Matthew's gospel: "Whatever you want men to do to you, do also to them, for this is the Law and the Prophets."[123] The underlying notion is "to do to others as you would have them do to you" or, put another way, "to treat others the same way you want them to treat you."

Confucius[124] applied the Golden Rule well in the marketplace: "What you do not wish for yourself, do not do to others … As you yourself desire standing, then help others achieve it; as you yourself desire success, then help others attain it." The Talmud similarly states: "What is hateful to you, do not to your fellow man. This is the law: all the rest is commentary." In the same way, Islam says: "None of you [truly] believes until he wishes for his brother what he wishes for himself."

The Golden Rule or ethic of reciprocity is a fitting code of morality found in most religions that looks at the issue in one of two ways:

- One should treat others as one would like others to treat oneself.
- One should not treat others in ways that one would not like to be treated.

This concept presupposes a 'reciprocal' or 'two-way' relationship between two parties that involves both sides equally, for their mutual benefit. The Golden Rule expresses it more as a matter of the heart and conscience. In his book, *50 Big Ideas You Really Need to Know*, Author Ben Duprẽ makes this point:

> *"It is the flouting of (moral consistency) – not practising what you preach –that makes hypocrisy so obnoxious. The basic objection to ... the politician who takes a backhander while fulminating against financial impropriety is inconsistency: between their stated opinions and the beliefs that are evinced by their behavior; between the importance they claim to attain to certain propositions and the indifference that one can infer from their actions."*[125]

We're all familiar with those who stridently advocate one thing with their words, then do something entirely different in their daily lives. Most of us prefer to spend only as much time as is necessary with such people, because not only do they not see the error of their way, but they have no use for those who dare mention it. But if we hate this behavior so much, why do we deal with them at all? Perhaps if we all left in protest, leaving them in isolation, they might take the hint and change their ways. The same idea holds merit, whether in personal life or in business.

The well-known quote from Edmund Burke has never held more truth than it does today: "The only thing necessary for the triumph of evil is for good men to do nothing."[126]

The Golden Rule is, in essence, a moral injunction that, if applied, will bode very well for the marketplace according to biblical principles, one in particular: "... for whatever a man sows, that he will also reap."[127] By implication, if an organization sows unfairness and cruelty, it will inevitably bring about its own demise, while sowing fairly and with compassion can only reap greater rewards.

Christianity is the only religion that goes further than the Golden Rule, which I refer to as the 'rule of rules.'

The Rule of Rules

Though there are 613 rules and regulations found in the Old Testament Jewish Law and the Ten Commandments, Jesus really simplified matters in His reply to a lawyer, a Pharisee, on the greatest command in the law:

"You shall love the Lord your God with all your heart, with all your soul, and with all your mind. This is the first and great commandment. And the second is like it: 'You shall love your neighbour, as yourself.'"

The issue is not complicated. *Love God and love people.* The lawyer addressed by Jesus was trying to trap Him. But instead of giving the hypocritical Pharisees a loophole that allowed them to obey one commandment while ignoring the rest, Jesus summed up all the commandments of God in two simple sentences: *Love God* and *love your neighbour*. If you truly love your neighbour, you won't steal from him, and you won't exploit or plunder him.

With that simple answer, Jesus refused to acknowledge the lawyer's cleverness and gave him no wiggle room to ignore the essential purpose of the law. Instead of demanding that he keep all 613 laws, or even the Ten Commandments, Jesus condensed it down to two simple commands: *love God and love people.*

I've been fortunate to encounter many individuals who genuinely live out the greatest commandment. Particularly concerning those who are outside my biological family, I'm indebted to many people and especially grateful to my British ministry leader and his wife, as well as to a sister in Christ who faithfully and very regularly prays for my family.

Sadly, there has been a steady decline in trust amongst the participants in the marketplace, which distrust is due in part to what I call a decline in SEPA.

SEPA

SEPA is the acronym I have given to the gracious human emotions collectively referred to as sympathy, empathy, pity, and altruism. These terms are clearly defined by Szalavitz & Perry in their book *Born for Love: Why Empathy is Essential – and Endangered:*[128]

> *"When you <u>empathize</u> with someone, you try to see and feel the world from his or her perspective. Your primary feelings are more related to the other person's situation than your own. But when you <u>sympathize</u>, while you understand what others are going through, you don't necessarily feel it yourself right now, though you may be moved to help nonetheless. <u>Pity</u> – or feeling sorry for someone – similarly captures this idea of recognizing another's pain without simultaneously experiencing a sense of it oneself. With empathy, however, you feel the other person's pain. You're feeling sorry 'with' them, not just 'for' them."*

The *Oxford English Dictionary* defines the terms this way:

<u>Sympathy</u>: *feelings of pity and sorrow for someone else's misfortune.*

<u>Empathy</u>: *the ability to understand and share the feelings of another.*

<u>Pity</u>: *the feeling of sorrow and compassion caused by the sufferings and misfortunes of others.*

185

<u>Altruism</u>: *selfless concern for the well-being of others.*

Selflessness or altruism is the practice of concern for the welfare of others. It is a traditional virtue in many cultures and a core aspect of various religious traditions, though the notion of 'others' (beneficiaries of such concern) varies among cultures and religions. This quality is the opposite of selfishness.

Altruism is distinctly different than simple feelings like duty and loyalty. It is the motivation to provide something of value to someone other than one's self, while duty strictly focuses on a moral obligation to a particular individual or group. Pure altruism requires the sacrifice of time, energy, or possessions for someone other than oneself, expecting nothing in return.

In combination, the SEPA qualities mesh to become grace in its finest form - a beautiful quality to observe. Grace is able to walk in another person's shoes and reach out to bless him/her, and to be blessed in return. Can you imagine the outcome if grace were added to business endeavours across the globe?

The failure to understand and cultivate grace, if left unchecked, will ultimately lead to a society where nobody wants to live - a cold, violent, chaotic, and terrifying world, where there is no warmth, only animosity and alienation. In the marketplace, grace is a very rare and precious commodity. Grace is the clean air we now need to breathe in the polluted marketplace, and THE point of this book. The marketplace will become a sad and destitute place until we elevate grace to 'treasure' status.

Consider the feeling of nostalgia many of us get remembering how our parents and grandparents lived, with far more grace, in spite of low incomes and few material possessions. At the time of the Great Depression, desperate unemployed men often walked or hopped trains, going from town to town, seeking work, and when there was none, they knocked on the doors of the locals to ask for food. While the housewife who answered the door had a place to call home, she often had to be quietly creative to feed her family. But even then, most were willing to give hungry strangers a bite to eat. What about now - do we even open our doors to strangers?

Listen to the wisdom of Proverbs 11:23-24: "The desire of the righteous is only good, but the expectation of the wicked is wrath. There is one who scatters, yet increases more; and there is one who withholds more than is right, but it leads to poverty."

Kindness

Merriam-Webster Dictionary defines the word 'kindness' as "the quality or state of being kind." According to Wikipedia, kindness is "the act or the state of being kind, being marked by good and charitable behavior, pleasant disposition, and concern for others." It is regarded as a virtue, and acknowledged as a value in many cultures.

Did you notice the phrases "charitable behavior" and "pleasant disposition" in the definition above? How often these days do we see those kinds of people? In this regard, comedic actor Charlie Chaplin aptly said: "We think too much and feel too little. More than machinery, we need humanity. More than cleverness, we need kindness and gentleness."

Kindness is one of the seven Contrary Virtues derived from an epic poem written by Prudentius[129] where practicing these virtues is believed to protect from temptation to the Seven Deadly Sins: *kindness* against envy, *humility* against pride, *abstinence* against gluttony, *chastity* against lust, *patience* against anger, *liberality* against greed, and *diligence* against sloth.

Kindness, like empathy, is to have compassion and understanding for someone else's plight, while protecting your own boundaries. Kindness reaches out to help someone else, not merely to make itself look good, but from a genuine compassion for your neighbor. Sometimes kindness is difficult, and can at times require us to say, "No," when it's necessary for the other person to face the consequences of their actions and learn valuable life lessons.

I recall the time I was once invited by an attorney for lunch after spending a small fortune in fees with his firm, only to charge me an additional $1,500 for the time he took to enjoy lunch with me. Clearly, we immediately started to look for a kinder attorney firm.

Conversely, I've found that the virtue of kindness transcends religious boundaries. I share a warm relationship with numerous Muslim individuals who consistently treat me with generosity and hospitality. One especially memorable example is an elderly Muslim family man in Cape Town who, without exception, calls me every year on my birthday - a heartfelt gesture that continues to reflect his enduring kindness.

Robert Burns[130] was correct: "[It is] the heart benevolent and kind that most resembles God." It was once said that one kind act will teach more love of God than a thousand sermons. The kindest are those who forgive and forget.

Think back to the times when others treated you with unusual kindness? These rare individuals stand out in vivid relief against the background of a harsh reality, don't they? Your simple acts of kindness will do the same for others, and God will be well pleased that we are attending to a needy soul.

Goodwill

One day, a young boy was misbehaving while his father was Christmas shopping. In irritation, the father threatened, "If you don't stop, I'll give all your Christmas presents to Goodwill." The son frowned: "Who's Will?"

The term 'goodwill' denotes an attitude of kindness, friendliness, or benevolence (a disposition to do good). At the same time, business conduct is most often characterised by cold, calculating behavior motivated by selfishness. As hard as it is to believe, the vice of greed has recently become celebrated in the marketplace as a virtue. Unfortunately, such an atmosphere makes it much more difficult for benevolent individuals to succeed.

Ironically, this selfish profit motive is intrinsically at odds with the requirements of any moral code. If the business community is to sustain itself over the long haul, it must try to bring into balance business profits and moral compassion.

With that in mind, consider the kinds of movies that are so popular today. Like most good stories, they require some kind of tension, challenge, turmoil, or a 'bad guy' to create conflict. In fact, every good author knows he has no story without conflict. If we're honest, we must admit that we like them because we love to see the good guys win. However, this is the place where truth and fiction collide; it only appeals as long as it's happening to someone else, and the further removed, the better.

In fact, we want lives filled with peace and quiet, with little in the way of conflict, but that's rarely the way it is, apart from a massive injection of grace.

At this point, I fondly recall my school swimming coach, whose uncommon goodwill left a lasting impression on his students. Breaking swimming records became my way of showing gratitude for his immense support. In fact, even 43 years later, one of those records remains unbroken.

Favor

During the Middle Ages and the Renaissance, favors were given not just as a symbol of love but also as a display of friendship, allegiance, or as a reward for duties performed and services rendered.

Tokens and favors were given as payment for services that far outweighed the expectations of the king. For our purposes, a favor can be defined as a gesture of devotion and grace, a promise of more to come, or just simple loyalty between friends. It may also show appreciation, as when an award is given for good deeds done.

Obviously, it's not only impossible to acquiesce to all requests for help, but it's also foolish. However, instead of always refusing outright, it may be possible to compromise, saying, "I can't manage this project alone, but if you'll do this, I'll do that." Matching funds are an excellent example of this kind of compromise.

When occasions arise when you must completely refuse, you might want to explain your reasons, so as not to seem rude or uncooperative. Yet unreasonable or ridiculous requests are usually best answered with a simple, 'No.'

Many people assume that favors work as a kind of karmic bank account where, in the long term, you get out what you put in. But the reality is far more complex. For the most part, you should not expect people to automatically return favors. If you want something, you need to ask for it. Don't assume people will just help you out because you helped them. On the other hand, if you must resort to calling in a favor, the chances are that there is something lacking in the relationship.

Trading in a Graceless Environment

I wish to recount a few experiences my family and I have had that illustrate what it's like to operate in a graceless environment:

o I recall the time when my father was struck down with a heart attack while his five sons were young. His bank manager of many years visited him in the hospital, not to reassure him of financial support but to advise him that the bank was cancelling his financial overdraft protection because his creditworthiness was now in doubt.

   Grace acts otherwise - instead, it says, "I will reach out to others in their time of need."

o At one point, I spent many years as a foreigner in a country, building a business, paying high fees to many consultants and staff, yet I was rarely offered a cup of coffee in return.

   Grace acts otherwise - instead, it says, "May I offer you something warm to drink?"

o Some employees whom you dutifully look after will be the first to betray your trust and badmouth you.

   Grace acts otherwise - instead, it says, "I will speak the truth about your kindness and goodness."

o Some of our companies that were experiencing setbacks were charged outrageous and exaggerated professional fees.

Grace acts otherwise - instead, it says, "We will take pains to charge fair fees."

o At a difficult time when one of our companies was showing steep losses, the Managing Director of the company requested a bonus for his services, failing which "he will leave the company with its problems."

Grace frowns at this conduct. Instead, it offers "to take a salary cut and remain at the post during a vulnerable time for the company."

o Devoting significant time and resources to developing one of our leaders, only for him to launch his own business using the intellectual property gained during their tenure.

After observing the misconduct, Grace is inspired to uphold to higher standards.

o When company leaders fail to promptly acknowledge and reward the hard work of their staff.

Grace takes the initiative to thoroughly identify company savings with the goal of using them to enhance staff welfare.

o When CEOs travel in 'business class,' while some of their colleagues commute on foot or by bicycle.

Grace simply always travels 'economy class' as a sign of respect to their colleagues, even if it's intercontinental flights.

o When leaders are disheartened by a perceived lack of respectful acknowledgment from their colleagues.

Grace has no need to receive 'acknowledgement.' Grace extends 'acknowledgements'

o A Director of one of our companies once invited me for lunch to inform me that he thought it was a better marketing idea to remove the word 'God' from all our literature, which is more commercially acceptable.

This has nothing to do with commerce; the request was dishonorable to God.

o A disabled employee who works for our company once hitchhiked many miles on a Saturday to our Head Office, just to deliver a box of chocolates to my father as a birthday gift.

This is a stunning example of grace.

o At one time, a swarm of locusts attacked the harvest of one of our farms. Contrary to the rest of nature, when a locust swoops down, it strips everything before moving on. Upon seeing this horrifying sight, my father and brother fell to their knees and prayed, and as a result, the locusts took flight, leaving minimal damage.

This is a prime example of God's supernatural grace.

In times of crisis, grace does not ask, "What can you do for me?" Instead, it says, "What can I do for you?" We ought to extend extra kindness whenever we get the chance.

Grace is such a significant subject of Scripture that we find both a parable on gracelessness and grace, together with a divine act of grace by the King Himself. Let's consider these.

A Parable of Gracelessness

Gracelessness is merely 'an act lacking grace,' the direct opposite of grace. In the Gospel of Matthew,[131] we find a parable of a man who knelt before the king to beg for more time to repay the 10,000 denarii he owed, so his wife and children would not be sold into slavery to pay the debt. As a result, the king was moved with compassion and forgave the servant his entire debt.

However, the ungrateful servant immediately pursued a debtor who owed him only 100 denarii (representing only 1% of the debt he himself had been forgiven) and threw the debtor into prison, ignoring the man's pleas for mercy. Although the unforgiving creditor had himself been forgiven a great debt, he refused to extend the same compassion to his debtor, but instead extended gracelessness. When the king heard about the man's selfish behavior, he threw him into jail, refusing to release him until he could pay off his own debt.

This parable exactly parallels the actions of many lending institutions, which themselves were rescued (by taxpayer money) during the banking crises from the brink of extinction, yet these institutions, in many cases, did not hesitate to foreclose on those taxpayers who owed a fraction of the debt they themselves had been forgiven.

When we act without compassion toward those around us, we leave a legacy of irreparable damage in our wake. Instead, each of us should play whatever part we can to lighten the load and loosen the yoke that enslaves others.

A Parable of Grace

In the parable of the workers in the vineyard of the landlord,[132] the landlord represents Jesus, the workers His followers, and the vineyard, His Kingdom. The salary of the workers stands for the rewards of salvation. The work is what His followers do to deserve the reward, and the day is the length of time they're given to do it, normally their lifespan.

In this parable, Jesus turns our concept of fair wages on its head. Some workers worked the entire day, whilst others were only employed for a fraction of the day. "So when evening had come, the owner of the vineyard said to his steward, 'Call the labourers and give them their wages, beginning with the last to the first.' And when those came who were hired about the eleventh hour, they each received a denarius. But when the first came, they supposed that they would receive more; and they likewise received each a denarius. And when they had received it, they complained against the landowner, saying, 'These last men have worked only one hour, and you made them equal to us who have borne the burden and the heat of the day.'"[133]

Jesus' parable makes no economic sense, and that was His intent. He was giving us a parable about grace, which cannot be determined in accounting terms. Grace is not about who worked the longest or hardest; it's about *not counting*. In the same way, we receive grace as a gift from God, not as something we toil to earn.

An Analogy of Grace

The Gospel of John introduces Jesus as the personification of grace: "For the law was given through Moses, but grace and truth came through Jesus Christ."[134] In one of His last acts before being crucified, Jesus extended divine grace to a thief dangling on a cross, the thief probably converting out of plain fear. That thief never attended synagogue or studied the Word of God at the time, and probably never made amends to all those he had wronged. He simply said, "Lord, remember me when You come into Your kingdom,"[135] and Jesus promised, "Assuredly, I say to you, today you will be with Me in Paradise."[136]

This well-known verse is another wake-up call that grace does not depend on what we have done for God but rather on what God has done for us.

Acts of Grace - Pay It Forward

An Iranian Poet aptly said: "Even after all this time, the sun never says to the earth, 'You owe me!' Look what happens with a love like that, it lights up the whole sky."[137]

The concept of 'pay(ing) it forward' (PIF) is an old one that asks the beneficiary of a good deed to repay it to others instead of to the original benefactor. PIF is at times implemented in contract law with regard to loans to third-party beneficiaries. Specifically, the creditor offers the debtor the option of paying the debt forward by lending it to a third person instead of paying it back to the original creditor. Payments can be made with either money or good deeds. A related type of transaction, which starts with a gift instead of a loan, is a good example of alternative giving.

The concept was described by Benjamin Franklin (Founding Father of the USA) in a letter to Benjamin Webb dated April 25, 1784:

"I do not pretend to give such a deed; I only lend it to you. When you [...] meet with another honest Man in similar Distress, you must pay me by lending this Sum to him; enjoining him to discharge the Debt by a like operation, when he shall be able, and all meet with another opportunity. I hope it may thus go thro' many hands, before it meets with a Knave that will stop its Progress. This is a trick of mine for doing a deal of good with a little money."[138]

A Hollywood movie, entitled *Pay It Forward*, is a worthy movie for anyone interested in the principles of grace. For individuals, these are some selfless ways you can pay it forward:

o   Partner with smaller or new businesses and support them by providing your skills or infrastructure where needed.

o   Host or sponsor networking or business events for local businesses.

- Identify budding entrepreneurs or start-up businesses and assist in 'business incubation'– give of your time and resources to get the business off the ground.
- Sponsor study opportunities by which people (young and old) are able to develop their skills.
- Offer free information workshops in your area or lend your expertise to your clients or members of the public.
- If you operate in the financial arena:
    - Assist students with guidance on how to save, invest, or do business.
    - Provide vocational guidance workshops to offer direction to young people.
    - Assist senior citizens regarding retirement planning.
    - Keep the account books for non-profit organizations or sports clubs, etc.
- Construct a link and open communications and facilitate relationships between the business world and non-profit organizations, like church groups.
- Support charities' non-profit endeavours with your time and money.
- Assist people or businesses in developing business plans for their businesses or business ideas.
- Provide your expertise to an existing community venture, either in coaching or administrating.

For Business Owners, some selfless ways to pay it forward:

o   Listen to someone's pain and help them find a path through it.

o   Buy small, inexpensive gifts for your clients on their birthdays.

o   Check up on someone who looks lonely.

o   Give your clients extra time to repay their debts.

o   Spread good news about your hardworking clients.

o   Give words of encouragement to every client about their dreams.

o   Set up donation boxes at your local businesses, and ask others to make contributions, to which you would donate one penny for every penny donated. Then, deliver the donations to those in need.

o   Take the time to teach someone a skill you know.

o   In your position of power, stand up for someone. Lend your voice. Often, the powerless, the homeless, and the neglected in our world need someone to speak up for them.

o   In some small way, when someone wants to repay you for something, ask them to pay it forward.

As a business leader, putting love in your decision-making is a very rewarding act, and it has nothing to do with your emotions. John Haggai had this to say about deciding with love: "How you feel is irrelevant. The love consists in the decision itself, not in how you felt when you made the decision. I can feel sorry for victims of an earthquake, but a far better barometer of my concern for them is whether I support efforts to help them."[139]

A Christian counsellor, David Seamands, summed up his career this way:

> "*Many years ago I was driven to the conclusion that the two major causes of most emotional problems among evangelical Christians are these: the failure to understand, receive, and live out God's unconditional grace and forgiveness; and the failure to give out that unconditional love, forgiveness, and grace to other people... We read, we hear, we believe in a good theology of grace. But that's not the way we live. The good news of the Gospel of grace has not penetrated the level of our emotions.*"[140]

Grace is a humbling yet uplifting presence that puts the perfect finishing touch on almost everything. Grace is, in essence, the heart of God, because every blessing we receive from Him was purchased for us at Christ's expense.

The Argument for Grace

Is it too much to expect that the high ethical ideal of grace could find itself in the dog-eat-dog marketplace? The strongest argument in favor of grace is the alternative, the existing graceless marketplace. The latter prospect is so painful to comprehend that considering actions to fracture gracelessness is the subject of the next chapter.

Interestingly, in this regard, consider that Chuck Colson, who perfected the art of power politics under the Nixon Administration, now says he has little faith in politics to solve the modern social problems. Instead, he points to acts of love or grace.[141]

Even if the marketplace demonstrated the highest standards of ethics or corporate governance, that would still fall wholly short of what is truly required in commerce. After all, the Pharisees in Jesus' day had impeccable ethics, and look what happened to them. Rather, Jesus gives us an important clue to improve commerce, which was when He reduced the mark of a Christian to one word: "By this all will know that you are My disciples, if you have love [i.e., have grace] for one another."[142]

It is often quoted that good is the enemy of great; that is certainly true for a secular marketplace. However, when it comes to the grace virtue, we must endeavour to be good more than great, and to serve the interests of others more than to advance our own. Learn to prefer grace to gold in all that you choose.

Summing up, we see that grace is not merely a virtue; it is a radical shift in posture, a courageous rejection of the transactional mindset that dominates the marketplace. As we step into a world where performance and profit reign supreme, choosing grace becomes an act of resistance, a divine disruption that restores humanity to commerce. Grace does not tally points or keep ledgers; it gives freely, forgives deeply, and serves without demand. And in doing so, it invites us to elevate not just our conduct but our calling.

To trade with grace is to partner with heaven's economy. The dividends of kindness, goodwill, and favor are not always measured on a balance sheet, but they are deeply felt in the hearts of those we touch. It is grace that breathes life into the cold mechanics of business, re-humanising systems that have lost sight of the people they were meant to serve. And perhaps that is the true gold of the marketplace - not what we accumulate, but what we extend.

Let us then be architects of a new kind of commerce, one built on compassion, guided by love, and anchored in grace. For in the end, grace is not weakness but power. It is not naiveté but wisdom. And it is not optional - it is essential. To choose grace is to choose legacy.

CHAPTER 8
FRACTURING UNGRACE

"Not by might nor by power, but by My Spirit."

(Zechariah 4:6)

Considering Ungrace

I was born into a family where my parents and grandparents taught and modelled *grace, a* virtue that stuck in my heart. I was taught by *Grace* for over 50 years, and God blessed me with my wife of 30 years, Almie, who exemplifies *grace.* For over thirty years, I also walked a path steeped in poison, void of grace - an airless realm where kindness wore no face. And to complete this harrowing design, I bore the bitter jest as though by fate's own line: the dubious honor for a considerable time with many a soul on malice bent.

The point I am trying to make is that through both blessings and trials long and lessons deep, I've come to truly see the tender light that grace bestows, and all its mystery. And just as clear, the monstrous shadow cast when grace is swept away. We must confront this beast called 'gracelessness,' not veil it in silence – it's yours and mine to defy.

The word 'gracelessness' lacks both dimension and depth, so for the rest of this chapter, I am rather going to refer to the term 'gracelessness' as 'ungrace,' which is an apt word used by Philip Yancey in his award-winning book: *What's so Amazing about Grace*. The word 'ungrace,' which is not a word included in *The Oxford English Dictionary*, is used here to denote the opposite of 'grace.'

One day, while travelling in the car with my father, he reminisced about the good old days when he was eighty, back at a time when he only needed to look at a fly, and the "irritating thing" would pass out. He then expressed his utter frustration, saying: "Today, you cannot merely use Doom [poisonous gas] to kill the thing. Now you have to smack it, jump on it, and then beat it with a broom." I was amused to hear my usually reserved father express his passion to such a degree, that said, I can't help but share the same feelings about ungrace. It is much like an irritating fly, and in this case, poisonous gas ain't going to eliminate it (which implies we need a much more powerful weapon to destroy it).

In 1998, I had a vivid dream of a dam that had a fortress of walls around it. It was an impactful dream with many symbolisms, where I was personally under intense attack beneath the dam walls with army tanks and soldiers bombarding me from every side. When I landed under an army tank in the dream, I noticed a crack in the dam wall, which soon split and crumbled so that a tsunami of water exploded from its restraints, sweeping away dangerous forces.

Many years later, I woke suddenly at 4 a.m. in my hotel room in Singapore, as if shaken awake by the Holy Spirit. After many years, unable to interpret the 1998 dream, it was clear that the meaning of this specific dream was to be revealed. My dream was similar to King David's experience as recorded in 2 Samuel 5 when the Lord instructed him to go up against the Philistines in battle. When David defeated his enemies, he exclaimed: "The LORD has broken through my enemies before me, like a breakthrough of water."[143] At that time, God miraculously manifested Himself to David as the King of the breakthrough. On behalf of David and his army, God in the Spirit burst forth through the enemy lines of the Philistines just like water breaks through a dam.

In my dream, the dam was symbolic of ungrace hindering the saving grace of God in the workplace. And there I was in battle at the foot of the dam wall, just as I do today and every other day in the marketplace. However, I noticed a slight fracture in the dam wall, and understood thereby the need for society to fracture

206

ungrace so that the walls will crumble under the pressure of the water, which symbolizes the power of the Holy Spirit.

Let me explain further the story I was told of a talk show host who invited five religious leaders to sit on a panel to discuss important life issues. The five leaders held vastly different points of view, but all eagerly accepted his invitation. As the host confronted each leader about the tough questions we face today, every leader except the Christian leader gave wise and clever answers.

The series of questions was repeated several times to give each person several chances to respond, yet each time the Christian leader failed to impress the audience. As a result, the Christians in the audience were clearly disappointed by the poor response from their representative. At the end of the show, the host congratulated the leaders for their excellent responses, but confronted the Christian for his unimpressive answers to which the Christian duly replied: "Sir, I don't have the answers to all of life's issues, but I just want to say to that woman in the wheelchair sitting in the front row, believe in the name of Jesus and you can rise up and walk." Instantly, the woman stood and began to walk, shocking the now-silent crowd of naysayers.

Christianity is wholly dependent on the power and authority of the Holy Spirit to "heal the brokenhearted, to proclaim liberty to the captives, and the opening of the prison to those who are bound."[144] Revival is coming to the marketplace, but we have a duty to do before the dam walls explode and the healing power of the Holy Spirit is released. In fact, because God gave us His authority on earth, we must have the faith to believe God's promises and speak them into being as if they are already ours. As faith precedes power, so too must we use faith to fracture ungrace, in preparation for revival. We therefore must pray to fracture ungrace, to bring forth a new revival of grace in the marketplace.

Does the Christian emphasis on grace have any relevance in the marketplace where evil forces and ungrace prevail? Yes, it most certainly does, and the following arguments are the reasons why.

Fracturing with Forgiveness

In 1990, the world watched a drama of forgiveness enacted on the stage of world politics. After East Germany chose a parliament in its first free elections, their first official act was to unanimously adopt the following position:

> *"We, the first freely elected parliamentarians of the GDR.... on behalf of the citizens of this land, admit responsibility for the humiliation, expulsion, and murder of Jewish men, women, and children. We feel sorrow and shame, and acknowledge this burden of German history.... Immeasurable suffering was inflicted on the peoples of the world during the era of national socialism.... We ask all the Jews of the world to forgive us. We ask the people of Israel to forgive us for the hypocrisy and hostility of official East*

German policies toward Israel and for the persecution and humiliation of Jewish citizens in our country after 1945 as well."[145]

In a similar world drama of forgiveness, Nelson Mandela emerged from nearly twenty-seven years of imprisonment with an unexpected and hopeful message of forgiveness and reconciliation, rather than demanding revenge.

These two powerful world events teach us unequivocally that the chains of ungrace can indeed snap and will break in commerce, but the fracturing process begins with acts of forgiveness. If grace holds such incredible power in politics, it will change the world, also wielding power in the marketplace. The fact that a diplomatic relationship exists at all between Germany and Israel, and that peaceful elections took place in South Africa when apartheid was dismantled, are stunning demonstrations of the power of grace and its counterpart, forgiveness.

Colossians 3:13 explains the work of forgiveness and reconciliation this way: "[Bear] with one another, and forgiving one another, if anyone has a complaint against another; even as Christ forgave you, so you also must do." I don't believe secular sources like dictionaries can adequately define the multifaceted term we call 'forgiveness,' because it is supernatural in nature. And because of its complexity, it requires divine guidance and empowerment, simply to go against our inherent humanity to make it happen.

We just need to consider the terrible actions of Robert Mugabe, Zimbabwe's president for over thirty years, to understand the consequences of harnessing the power of ungrace – 80% unemployment, 231 million percent peak hyperinflation, widespread murder, and the collapse of the rule of law. You just need to visit Harare International Airport to witness the ramifications of the polluted fumes of ungrace on individuals – devastating dejection and the complete loss of dignity that has decimated an entire culture.

John Hagee once said, "When you forgive someone, you totally free yourself from the person's power to control you." Joyce Meyer says, "Un-forgiveness is like drinking poison and hoping someone else would die." These are tough words, but they help us understand that forgiveness not only fractures ungrace, but it also has the redeeming quality of un-poisoning and restoring our lives.

In physical terms, such 'un-poisoning' is associated with a lower heart rate and blood pressure, as well as relieving stress. It is also associated with alleviating physical symptoms, reducing fatigue, and improving the quality of restorative sleep. In the psychological realm, forgiveness is associated with lower stress while simultaneously restoring positive thoughts, feelings, and behaviors.[146]

George Herbert gave one of the most powerful arguments in favor of forgiveness when he made this statement: "He that cannot forgive others, breaks the bridge over which he himself must pass."

So urgent is the need for forgiveness that Jesus repeatedly gave it precedence over mere religious duties: "Therefore, if you bring your gift to the altar, and there remember that your brother has something against you, leave your gift there before the altar, and go your way. First be reconciled to your brother, and then come and offer your gift."[147]

Fracturing by Being Nice

Our family business has interviewed thousands of potential candidates for job vacancies. One constant variable throughout these interviews was that the candidates all presented themselves either as intellectual or quite competent, with high levels of integrity. Our concluding remark would mostly be: "But are you nice?" which usually earned us little more than a blank stare.

Our company made it our policy; we cherished compassion and being user-friendly at the top of our list. Simply put, we tried to convey to our colleagues the vital importance of 'being nice.' In the end, our hunch was right (it was my hunch but my father's insistence); amiable, compassionate people stayed in the company, and they were not only popular but also far more profitable in the long run.

What do I mean by the terms 'being nice' or 'user-friendly'? By that I mean someone who offers courtesy, politeness, and good character, not a control freak, a psychopath, or bad-tempered. And while we don't require our employees to put up with foolishness, neither do we make excuses for divisive behavior or rudeness, which are unequivocally toxic to good relationships, whether personal or in business settings.

The power of niceness was confirmed in a research report by Harvard University. In essence, the report plainly proved that it pays to be nice.[148] It is often assumed that screaming coaches and ruthless business tycoons are big winners in their respective fields. However, according to the Harvard report, that's not true at all; rather, nice people are the *"Victor Ludorums."*

The Harvard study involved ten college students playing a series of repeated games, a version of the prisoner's dilemma in game theory (I talk about game theory in Chapter 2). Researchers discovered that increasingly competitive players who escalated the level of conflict during the games very often found themselves ruined by the end of the game. The research found a definite correlation between punishment and profit. The players who punished opponents the least, or not at all, ultimately made the most profit. The lesson to be learned from this valuable research is that it's in our best interest to be 'nice.'

While regulators are necessary and important institutions designed to govern conduct in the marketplace, when the power goes to their heads, they can make life miserable for those under their care. Truly, if a Chieftain within that institution does not like your accent or world view, but instead loves the power that the institution provides, then that individual will unleash the fury of hell over you just to prove a point. If regulators started treating people like human beings rather than animals, the ugly ducklings (the marketplace individual) would strive to become swans simply to impress their bosses (the regulators). However, when you are always treated like an ugly duckling, you have less motivation to transform into the swan you have always longed to be. Nevertheless, still strive to become the swan you have always longed to be!

Hatred and anger are powerless when met with niceness. John Wesley summed up being nice very succinctly: "Do all the good you can. By all the means you can. In all the ways you can. In all the places you can. At all times, you can. To all the people you can. As long as ever you can."

Fracturing by Caring

Before considering how we can fracture ungrace by caring, let's first address the difference between the virtues of 'caring' and 'being nice.' A review of the word 'nice person' generally refers to a person who is kind, polite, warm, helpful, friendly, and considerate. The term 'caring' has the aspects of 'nice' and generally refers to displaying concern for others. Although the two terms are quite similar, a truly caring person goes further than merely being 'nice,' the person also offers sincere compassion.

This book has much to say about the conduct of Chieftains, who are mostly found in leadership positions or authoritative positions. The problem is that, over time, Chieftains tend to forget that they have been given a sacred trust in which the well-being of others is placed in their care. Too many habitually abuse this sacred responsibility for personal ends. James Autry explained this sacred trust very well: "It is a trust placed upon [Chieftains] first by those who put [them] in the job, but more important than that, it is a trust placed upon [them] after [they] get the job by those whom [they] are to manage."[149]

Our success rate for acquiring new hospitality clients was not less than 7/10, with a simple strategy: we show that we care, and we are genuine about it. If we can simply forget balance sheets and intellect and just be genuine about caring, we will win over the client. It's true, everyone loves to be loved.

Unfortunately, there is no simple list of rules or things to do to show you care, but the following are a few ideas that worked in our enterprises:

o   Rather than talking about oneself or what the business could do, take an interest in the client;

o   Say very little and make every attempt to listen intently to the clients' needs. Listening is a gift of grace and kindness;

o   Rarely say "No" to the client. Instead, try to respond with: "Yes" or "I will do my best, and if I can't help, I will refer you to someone I believe can address your issues." This response takes the weight off the clients' shoulders, and you let them know you are in the situation with them;

o It remains very effective to telephone clients on their birthdays. Emails on birthdays are not worthwhile;

o Make a point to show an interest in the clients' family and their personal wellbeing, and personally, I was often present at the bedside of an ailing grandmother;

o Show respect to your client by being on time for meetings, which lets them know you appreciate both their valuable time and their business;

o Make it your mission to be a problem-solver, because people highly value problem-solvers.

o Philippians 2:3: "Let nothing be done through selfish ambition or conceit, but in lowliness of mind let each esteem others better than himself."

Let me be frank for a moment: the truth is that in my experience, the people who really care are quick to express emotion. Babies moan but men of character sometimes cry.

There are numerous ways we can fracture ungrace by caring, but this book can only consider the subject briefly. However, I would like to mention one more core matter of caring, and that's a genuine commitment to the job.

"A good way to think about commitment is as dedication to the work a person has chosen to do. Not as dedication to a job. The difference is not frivolous, because it goes to the heart of an employee's attitude about what he or she does."[150] By way of analogy, if someone loves being a manager (loves the job prestige of being a department head), that is far different than a manager who loves motivating others to work together to accomplish specific goals (loves the work).

Over the years, I have experienced that people get dismissed more often from situations where they loved the job, but only rarely from situations where they loved the work. The point here is that commitment to work leads more readily to caring attitudes.

No better example is given of the virtue of caring than that exemplified by Apostle Paul. At a time when the Philippians neglected for a time to enquire after him and neglected to send him any presents, instead of chastising them for their neglect, he makes an excuse for them in Philippians 4:10: "though you surely did care, but you lacked opportunity." The Apostle is willing to suppose, in favor of them, that they would have cared for him if given a fair opportunity. A most remarkable heart attitude, that's why Christ called him to the office of Apostleship!

Fracturing by Changing the Metaphors

A metaphor is "a figure of speech in which a word or phrase is applied to an object or action to which it is not literally applicable"[151] – as illustrated by this phrase – "The amounts of money being lost by the company were enough to make it a metaphor for an industry that was teetering."

The marketplace tends to pay far more attention to its jargon than to metaphors, and it's been my experience that it places little emphasis on words unless litigation is imminent. Scripture, however, cautions us regarding the incredible power of words. Proverbs 18:21 says that "Death and life are in the power of the tongue, and those who love it will eat its fruit." Ephesians 4:29 further admonishes that "Let no corrupt word proceed out of your mouth, but what is good for necessary edification, that it may impart grace to the hearers."

James Autry explains it well: "Becoming a manager has much to do with learning the metaphors; becoming a good manager has much to do with using the metaphors; and becoming a leader has much to do with changing the metaphors."[152] I am dedicating a bit more time to this issue because it is so sadly neglected.

How can we fracture ungrace by changing the metaphors? By that, I don't mean to imply that it's enough to merely change the metaphors, because it's also necessary to choose our words more carefully and with grace. When a company makes this statement: "Relationships are our biggest asset," the company is either lying or using a metaphor to change the perceptions of its employees and its customers. I don't believe companies would purposely lie when making such a statement. Still, the outcome hinges on whether or not the company's leaders understand both the value of good relationships and the impact of their spoken words.

By making the statement that "relationships are our biggest asset," the company's leadership understands that relationships are inherently difficult to manage but also realizes that things and people become what we call them, and that truly death and life are in the power of the tongue. In the marketplace, words can work magic and change perceptions, improving morale and increasing sales. On the other hand, words can wreak havoc if not seasoned with grace.

For a moment, let's consider the negative and positive effects of words and metaphors:

Statement A: "I don't think your work is particularly good. Do it over." This statement implies that the person is inept, incapable of doing the job.

Statement A rephrased: "I don't think your work is complete; you can do better." This statement implies that the person is quite capable of doing better work. Such wording inspires the employee with hope and encouragement.

Statement B: "That company is going to collapse." Many make this type of irresponsible statement to the detriment of the company, only adding fuel to the potential fire of destruction.

Statement B rephrased: "That company is going through a very difficult time, but it has the human talent to survive." Even if the truth is negative, it can still be said in a positive way, to offset the negative and encourage hope.

Statement C: "Travel agencies are a dying industry." This implies that travel agencies are worthless and no longer useful.

Statement C rephrased: "I like using travel agencies, although they need to better address the needs of e-commerce." If you blindly book your next holiday via the web instead of using a proficient travel agent, then you will learn firsthand the value extended by travel agents.

Statement D: "The boss is a lunatic who always demands his own way." This implies that the boss is someone who cannot be trusted and might even be emotionally unbalanced.

Statement D rephrased: "I have a difficult boss, but he always makes sure that I get paid on time." This implies that although the boss is not perfect, he is fair.

Statement E: "Never do business with family or friends." Well, this is so often said, but it's just foolish talk. Would you rather give preference to work with a stranger?

Taking care to use the most appropriate and upbeat words shows that you are aware that words have power and that you do not wish to prejudge a situation to another's ruin. If you're still in doubt, let me tell you a true story I once heard:

A young man was sitting down on the only bench at a bus stop. An elderly woman arrived at the bus stop and uttered irate words when the young man did not immediately offer her his seat. The woman suddenly took her walking stick and poked the young man with it, to which he replied, "Oh, I'm terribly sorry, Ma'am. I did not mean to be inconsiderate. I've been sitting here trying to absorb the news that my daughter was injured in a car accident."

We must never react, assuming the worst or judging hidden motives that we do not know or understand. Instead, we must realize there may be extenuating circumstances which have nothing to do with us, for which we can choose to make allowances. Until we walk a mile in another's shoes, we never know what another person is going through.

Fracturing by Equanimity

The word 'equanimity' is interesting, defined by Merriam-Webster online dictionary as "evenness of mind especially under stress." The philosophical stance is that you cannot control others, only your reaction. When treated unjustly, equanimity calls for a patient response, viewing the situation as a chance to strengthen resilience and uphold one's integrity.

In the section above, I included a quote from James Autry on changing the metaphors, which I am slightly going to rephrase for the philosophical stance of equanimity:

"Becoming a manager has much to do with learning the virtue of equanimity; becoming a good manager has much to do with being patient with your response to a hostile environment; and becoming a leader has much to do with your attitude to view hostile situations as a forum to strengthen resilience and uphold one's integrity."

I try not to always invoke my father, though it's difficult not to. He was my mentor and the one who introduced me to the rare concept of 'equanimity.' I still don't fully understand how he maintained it in the hostile environments he endured, but to me, he embodied it flawlessly — a perfect 10/10 in grace under pressure. And then my mother - she edged him out in the end, earning a bonus point in this regard. A perfect 10.5/10. And then me - well, I'm still working on my points …

Let me illustrate with a practical example. I was once with my father in a tense meeting involving our building construction team members. I had made a careless decision that put others at significant risk of construction delays. My father, however, responded with quiet, diplomatic resilience - not to preserve his own standing, but to shield me from becoming completely disheartened by my mistake. Without a word of blame, he immediately covered the cost of the wasted time and left the meeting as though nothing had happened. He understood that I had already learned the lesson, and he had no desire to compound the mistake with shame or injury. That moment taught me a great deal, and I have now memorialized it in this book as a powerful example of equanimity in action.

Fracturing by Doing the Right Thing

In the 1990s, the U.S. Library of Congress named Dr. Victor Frankl's ground-breaking work, *Man's Search for Meaning*, as one of the ten most influential books of the twentieth century.[153] An Austrian psychiatrist and Jewish Holocaust survivor, Dr. Frankl was a heroic figure, not only for his profound writing ability and insight into the human condition, but also for his great personal integrity. More than once during times of crisis, he put himself in mortal danger, risking his own life to protect or care for others. He made this profound statement:

> *"Being human always points, and is directed, to something or someone, other than oneself – be it a meaning to fulfil or another human being to encounter. The more one forgets himself, by giving himself to a cause to serve or another person to love, the more human he is ... [Such a person] knows the 'why' for his existence, and will be able to bear almost any 'how.'"*[154]

As mentioned earlier, it is possible to fracture ungrace by doing the right thing: doing good as much as you can, as often as you can, to as many people as you can. Those whose goals focus on merely attaining 'happiness' generally seek it for themselves alone. They want to feel good and are most often 'takers' rather than 'givers.' Both Scripture and Dr. Frankl encourage us not to seek 'happiness' but 'meaning,' which focuses on giving and self-sacrificing for the benefit of others. I like Stephen Swecker's definition of living with meaning:

> "*To live a meaningful life is to live in conscious relationship with core values that command our allegiance, summon our energies, and call us out of ourselves to a sense of responsibility for something greater than ourselves.*"[155]

Doing the right thing is not simply about thinking the right thoughts; it requires actions that focus on the well-being of others. We need to base our lives on the moral compass inherently inside us, because we are all born in the image of God, which factors in a much broader view of what makes life worth living. A life void of grace is a catastrophe in the making, so we need to fracture any evidence of ungrace, one action at a time. In fact, several studies have shown that life is far more rewarding if it is focused on others.

I was once faced with the weighty decision of deciding for strangers at the cost of my lifelong professional dream. When the Holy Spirit guided me on what it meant to make the right choice, albeit outvoted by my Swiss Board, I sacrificed the dream at great personal and substantial financial cost from the repercussions that followed. When doing the right thing, it often involves the well-being of strangers. I am grateful I obeyed, and I encourage you to make the unselfish decision for the goodwill of others.

Fracturing with Humility

The marketplace often disdains humility, encouraging bold aggressiveness instead. But what do I mean when I use the word 'humility' in this instance? First, we need to realize that it's the opposite of a haughty spirit as referred to in Proverbs 16:18, "Pride goes before destruction, and a haughty spirit before a fall."

This kind of humility is based on inner strength of character, where there is inherent confidence in God while having a modest view of one's own importance. This attitude understands that it doesn't need to force itself forward because God will make a place for it. The humble person makes a consistent effort to follow the rule: "Be kindly affectionate to one another with brotherly love, in honor giving preference to one another."[156]

Humility sees with the eyes of wisdom where pride would blind us - to the needs of others as well as to our own shortcomings. The media and the marketplace generally consider humility a weakness, but this is not what Jim Collins found and documented in his book entitled *Good to Great*. In it, he explains why certain businesses catapulted past their competitors to greatness and profiled 'Level 5 Leaders' who were at the helm of every company on his list. He says that this type of leader is "an individual who blends extreme personal humility with intense professional will."[157]

To quote Collins: "It's not that Level 5 leaders have no ego or self-interest. Indeed, they are incredibly ambitious – but their ambition is first and foremost for the institution, not themselves."[158] One of the most famous Level 5 leaders is Nelson Mandela, who, after his release from jail, averted civil war in South Africa by his acts of forgiveness and humility, yet embodied a strong character. Was Mother Teresa weak because she was so humble? Absolutely not! She was extraordinarily stubborn in her single-minded focus to serve the poor, no matter what it cost her personally.

In a study of the leadership of companies that went from just good to great, humility was found to play a significant role.[159] In this study, eleven of the 1,435 companies that made the Fortune 500 between 1965 and 1995 were identified as exceptional. Humility was identified as a key trait of the CEOs of each of the outstanding eleven companies. In fact, humility was associated not only with a better quality of social relationships because others perceived the leaders as well-adjusted and kind, but it was also linked with many pro-social behaviors, including gratitude, forgiveness, and cooperation.

Humility is the product of tough times and develops resilience in the fires of adversity. Adversity teaches us that God is sovereign and all-powerful, infinite in wisdom, which means that walking in humility before God is the only wise way to do things. From the biblical account of Joseph's imprisonment, we discover an object lesson that God used hardships to intentionally root out an individual's rebellion to instill a profound humility of heart and dependence on God. True meekness comes when we see that on our own, we are nothing and therefore submit so that God can be everything to us.

These are wise words on humility in the marketplace from Jonathan Edwards:

> "*Some persons are always ready to level those above them down to themselves, while they are never willing to level those below them up to their own position. But he that is under the influence of true humility will avoid both these extremes. On the one hand, he will be willing that all should rise just so far as their diligence and worth of character entitle them to; and on the other hand, he will be willing that his superiors should be known and acknowledged in their place, and have rendered to them all the honors that are their due.*"[160]

I have seen countless instances of cursing in the marketplace. Remember that no matter who you are, you cannot curse without facing severe consequences. In the same way, you cannot win with pride and an arrogant spirit because this is one of the seven attributes God hates above all others.[161]

Fracturing by Faith

The marketplace has suffered deep scars from the toxic effects of ungrace. We are in desperate need of faith that is authentic and transforms every area of the marketplace. Faith denotes a sense of trust or confidence placed in someone or something. The Bible defines faith as "the substance of things hoped for, the evidence of things not seen."[162] It also says that by faith, "the elders obtained a good testimony."[163]

Having someone or something to depend on is truly a stabilizing force amid the ups and downs of the marketplace. I am a Christian, so my faith is not in something but in Someone – the Triune God. Others have faith in government practices, so faith varies for all of us. However, for the purpose of this book, the faith I refer to "is complete trust in God, even in the absence of reason."

Perhaps you've heard the saying, "Failure and victory are both in the mind." There is a great deal of truth in this statement because the truth is that both success and failure originate in the belief system. In other words, if the mind has not completely written off a venture as a failure, there may still be hope for victory, but if the mind has already given up hope, failure becomes inevitable. This, in essence, is a good definition of faith — the power of the mind to believe in what may otherwise be impossible.

On the other hand, reason has no part in faith. Some people live their entire lives in the pursuit of something that reason prevents them from achieving. It is quite different with faith. When there is faith, there is no thought or worry regarding the means to accomplish the desire, so reason is simply not a deterrent. Jesus said to Peter, when he walked on the water, "O you of little faith, why did you doubt?"[164] If Peter had the faith, he could have done the impossible, defying both logic and physics, and conquered even the water.

Though many have discovered faith only as the result of crises, I was fortunate because, early on, faith became a way of life for me, partly because I had to endure many struggles. But faith never failed to give me purpose, and I consistently found myself intact and blessed rather than shattered in the face of adversity. Through faith, I always held onto the belief that God knew what was going on in my crisis and would turn it around for good as He promised, and He certainly did!

Let's consider the heroes of faith,[165] those who obtained a good testimony because of their faith. Enoch was translated to heaven so that he did not face death. Noah moved with godly fear and constructed an ark to save his household from certain death. Abraham obeyed God and was prepared to sacrifice his only son, and in return, he became the father of nations. By faith, when he was dying, Joseph made mention of the departure of the children of Israel and gave instructions concerning his bones. By faith, Moses led the Israelites through the Red Sea on dry land, while the Egyptians, attempting to do the same thing, were drowned by the walls of water crashing in on them. By faith, the harlot Rahab did not perish with those who did not believe, when she had received the spies with peace, and so on.

I also read a story of how even thieves honor faith, worthy for us to remember that faith transcends barriers:

The story is told of a young man who was traveling with a caravan through Arabia when they came to a place frequented by robbers, and everyone was advised to guard their belongings. The man thought to himself, "I have no place to keep my money. I will therefore find some man with whom I can entrust it for safekeeping."

So, he went and found a man smoking his pipe in a tent. He approached the man and said, "Excuse me, Sir. I do not know you, but I have heard there are thieves in the area and that many caravans have been robbed. I am a poor man, and felt that I must protect my money, if I could only find someone to whom I could entrust it. And when I found this tent, I felt I should entrust it to you." He left the purse and returned to the caravan. When he arrived, he found that it had been robbed, and everyone had lost their money.

When the young man rushed back to the tent to reclaim his money, he was shocked to learn that the man with whom he had left his money was the chief of thieves who had robbed the caravan. The man trembled and turned to run away without his purse, believing that he too would be victimized. But the thief shouted and demanded that the man return.

The Chief then addressed the young man: "Sir, I received your money to keep. I did not rob you of it. Because you trusted me, your money was therefore to my trust. Even if I am a robber, I am not dishonest. I gain by robbery, not by breaking trust. You trusted me with your money, and your money is safe. Here it is for you to take back again." As you can imagine, the man was delighted, reflecting on what a good thing trust is.

Step-by-Step

Many ways exist by which ungrace can be fractured. I have only mentioned seven virtues derived from the fruit of the spirit as contained in Galatians 5:22-23: "Love, joy, peace, longsuffering, kindness, goodness, faithfulness, gentleness, self-control." These virtues can be used to heap coals of fire on the heads of those who sow discord in the marketplace.

Every step we take to fracture grace, we will gradually see the crack enlarge in the dam, so that a small stream of water begins to seep through, loosening the dirt and enlarging the crack, so that in time the dam will utterly burst. The Holy Spirit will have His way, transforming the marketplace into a rare thing of beauty.

Fracturing ungrace is neither a grand crusade nor a singular heroic act — it is the consistent, everyday decision to respond with faith, humility, kindness, and care, even when the world offers us its opposite. It is easy to mirror the cruelty or indifference of the marketplace, but we are called to reflect something greater — a light that cuts through the smog of suspicion and selfishness. Ungrace cannot withstand the force of simple, consistent acts of love.

The cracks in the dam of ungrace are growing. Every time we forgive when revenge is easier, every time we speak with honor instead of judgment, every time we choose compassion over calculation, we weaken the stronghold. And as those cracks deepen, a flood of healing, of renewal, of divine presence is waiting to break through. That is the promise of grace: it transforms not by coercion, but by invitation. It changes not through might, but by the Holy Spirit.

May we be the ones who choose grace when it's costly, kindness when it's inconvenient, and faith when the odds are stacked against us. For when the dam breaks, and revival sweeps across the marketplace, it will not be because of strategies or slogans, but because ordinary people dared to live out extraordinary grace.

CHAPTER 9
DECODING THE MYSTERY

"Having made known to us the mystery of His will, according to His good pleasure which He purposed in Himself"

(Ephesians 1:9)

Solving the Complex

I've guided you through many twists and turns, shown different angles of the marketplace, as well as different defences and responses required from your attitude, all of which were necessary to prepare you to advance in decoding marketplace mysteries, i.e., resolving the complex problems you will face.

Problem solving with a secular mindset is very different from problem solving by prayer and faith. For the purposes of this chapter, I focus exclusively on the latter.

God is Sovereign and merciful; our limited understanding cannot comprehend the infinite depth, height, length, and breadth of His wisdom, so it's never possible to confine any Christian response to problem-solving to a formula or methodology. However, the Bible does make a clear connection between our spiritual condition (which includes 'works') and the effectiveness of our prayers (the Bible includes many verses in this regard; only a few are mentioned here):

Hear the instruction of 2 Timothy 2:12

> *"Be diligent to present yourself approved to God, a worker who does not need to be ashamed, rightly dividing the word of truth."*

Strengthen your hope from the direction of Romans 15:4

> *"For whatever things were written before were written for our learning, that we through the patience and comfort of the Scriptures might have hope."*

Righteousness is an essential component of answered prayer – James 5:16

> *"The effective, fervent prayer of a righteous man avails much."*

Sin (such as unforgiveness) creates a barrier between us and God – Isaiah 59:1-2

> *"Behold, the Lord's hand in not shortened, that it cannot save; Nor His ear heavy, that it cannot hear. But your iniquities*

have separated you from your God; and your sins have hidden His face from you, so that He will not hear."

Be guided by Jeremiah 32:17 when you wish to problem solve

"Ah, Lord God! Behold, You have made the heavens and the earth by Your great power and outstretched arm. There is nothing too hard for You."

In the preceding chapters, we studied the methodology of the marketplace, considered our defences, reflected on appropriate responses, and thereby we have taken steps to be "diligent to present ourselves approved to God." Very important first steps to initiate because we cannot please God without faith, and faith without works is dead. Assuming we have been diligent in the 'works' part, now let's consider various aspects of faith as they may apply practically in the marketplace:

Coding and Decoding like a King

To introduce this Kingdom Economic formula, as a starting point, let's consider Psalm 84:6:

"As they pass through the Valley of Baca, they make it a spring; The rain also covers it with pools."

The implied meaning of this verse is that the individual whose heart is set on the Lord digs a well, but strangely, this well fills from the top instead of only from the ground up. We dig a well, but the blessing of water to the well not only flows from the bottom but also from the top. Our efforts in labor (to dig the well) are tied to the end, but they do not of themselves produce it.

Taken from this Psalm, the rain covers the spring with pools of water (signifying abundance), so our efforts are not lost in creating the spring, but our labor does not supersede God's intervention in bringing the rain. Here's a Kingdom formula applied with faith:

<u>Elementary Math:</u> 1 unit of labor + 1 unit of labor = 2 units of labor

<u>Kingdom Math:</u> 1 + 1 ranging from 7 to infinity

With reference to Kingdom Math, Divine help is always a multiplier of our efforts/labor, so therefore applying the example of "1 unit of labor + 1 unit of labor," what do we get? I respectfully submit my reasoning -

o 1 + 1 cannot be equal to 2, because Divine help always supersedes labor

o Cannot be 2.1 because Kingdom Math works in whole numbers, not decimals

o Cannot be 3 because 3 represents [1 + 1 + (1) + (0)] as Divine help supersedes labor [i.e., here the "(1) + (0)" in brackets is not greater than "1 + 1"]

o Cannot be 4 because 4 represents [1 + 1 + (1) + (1)] as Divine help supersedes labor

- Cannot be 5 because 5 represents $[1 + 1 + (2) + (1)]$ as Divine help supersedes labor because the last "(1)" in brackets must be ">1.9"
- Next closest is only 6 $[1 + 1 + 2 + 2]$ as Divine help can only be a whole multiplier of labor $[1 + (1 \times 2)$ plus $1 + (1 \times 2)]$
- I don't believe the final number range is from 6 because, unlike mathematics, which is regarded as a 'precise science' due to its foundation on clearly defined concepts, strict logical reasoning, and exact rules, Kingdom Math surpasses the 'precise science' criteria. I submit the number in our example possibly 'ranges from' 7 because (i) it must be a whole number, and (ii) it likely may align with Biblical numerology (the number '7' in biblical numerology is among the most meaningful and symbolically profound numbers in the Bible, representing completeness and Divine order). I also purposefully use the expression 'ranges from' because we possibly cannot use the formula 'equal to' as the precise science criteria is absent.

As illustrated by Psalm 84:6, our efforts in labor are tied to the end sum in Kingdom Math, but once faith is added to our efforts, we get a surprisingly much greater total sum ranging from 7 to infinity. In fact, the estimated starting amount of 7 is quite conservative; the actual number is likely much greater. This is so because our minds struggle to grasp matters of faith; we can only explore the outer edges.

OK, what is the point I'm trying to make? It's an economic turning point, to be frank.

Since the marketplace only relies on math, the Kingdom mind is crucially different because it understands that the means of our labor with faith prayed into the equation will add a further dimension to the end result (multiply the end result of our labor).

For this reason, you must never look at your bank statement as the only indicator of what you have available, because with Kingdom math, $1 + 1$ is far greater than 2 ('2' representing your bank balance). This is not a theory to act in presumption where God hasn't provided guidance, but rather a firm reminder that faith brings a unique dimension to our thinking. I fully recognize that the naysayers and accountants are going to throw eggs at me for this statement. We respect their common-sense approach to reality, but for those with the eyes of faith, remember 'reality' and 'Faith' (purposefully written with a small 'r' and capital 'F') are two vastly different kingdoms.

To put Kingdom Math in another perspective, consider this:

A skeptic hiker got lost in the countryside and stumbled upon a farm. Desperate, he asked the Christian farmer for directions back to town.

The farmer said, "With pleasure. But first, come sit and have a bite. The Lord provides."

The skeptic scoffed, "With all due respect, I believe in facts and science, not invisible sky beings."

The gracious farmer smiled and handed him a steaming bowl of soup. "Fair enough. But tell me, if you are so sure there's no God, what do you say when you're in real trouble?"

The skeptic laughed, "I rely on logic and reason, not imaginary friends."

Just then, a bull from the field charged dangerously toward them. The skeptic screamed, "Oh God, help me!"

The farmer leaned on his tractor and thought to himself, "Funny how fast logic runs when a bull charges and only God is left standing."

Decision & Probability Asymmetry

'Decision asymmetry' is a useful concept that describes a scenario in which the individuals or groups involved in decision-making have unequal access to information, resources, authority, or exposure to risk, resulting in an imbalanced deliberation process or experience. The word 'asymmetry' refers to a lack of balance or equality – 'asymmetric information' is when one party in a transaction knows more than the other. Understanding this concept, matched with 'probability asymmetry,' provides surprising and profitable strategies.

The issue with decision asymmetry is that, in my experience, it often shows up during 'brainstorming' sessions, where there is usually a significant gap in individual participants' knowledge or experience. This imbalance tends to hinder, rather than help, the achievement of effective outcomes. Ah, but I had a moment of wisdom when I realized that my focus should not rest solely on the individuals involved, but also on the outcomes being pursued – leading to 'probability asymmetry.'

Let's consider 'probability asymmetry,' which refers to situations where the probabilities of different outcomes are not evenly distributed. Simply stated, by examining forex trading, the gains and losses have different 'weights,' even if the chances are the same. A practical example:

> You trade Euro/US$ at a time when there are an equal number of buyers and sellers, but you profit by $2 if the Euro appreciates, versus you only losing $1 if the Euro depreciates. Therefore, although the win/lose probability is 50/50, the win gain is much greater than the deficit of the loss – this is asymmetry.

2 Corinthians 9:6 has helped me conceptualize probability asymmetry. The verse states: "He who sows sparingly will also reap sparingly, and he who sows bountifully will also reap bountifully." It is my experience that the choices I made where I sowed sparingly (was not as compassionate as I should have been) resulted in say -1 (in terms of outcomes). In contrast,

the decisions I made where I sowed bountifully (was gracious in the decisions I made) were not a mere +1 but more like a +5 outcome.

Therefore, although decision asymmetry exists in most business settings, this, if balanced by a gracious mindset (characterized by generosity, empathy, humility, and goodwill), often produces disproportionately positive outcomes, particularly in human-centered contexts. A good example is when an employee underperforms or disagrees with leadership. Rather than reprimanding him, a leader who chooses to listen actively and offer mentorship can often inspire a remarkable transformation, turning the employee into a top performer or a loyal advocate.

Decision asymmetry with a gracious mindset often leads not only to better outcomes, but even if I am wrong just as often as I am right, I will still be on the better outcomes side of the curve.

Relativistic Insight

This hypothesis is inspired by *Albert Einstein's theory of relativity,* which proposes that space, time, and even the concept of simultaneity are fixed constants, but instead vary depending on the observer's motion and frame of reference. Relativistic insight is a deep form of knowledge that considers the shifting context, perspective, and conditions of a situation, acknowledging that good judgment or the best course of action can vary based on one's point of view.

After a bird strike disabled both engines of US Airways Flight 1549, Captain Chesley Sullenberger had only minutes to act. He made the split-second decision to land in the Hudson River instead of attempting to return to an airport. This was a classic case of relativistic insight because the Captain defied air traffic control's advice and managed to land the plane safely without any casualties, making a decision that demanded sound judgment in an intense, high-pressure situation.

Another notable example occurred in 1940, when, after France's fall left Britain isolated, many urged negotiating peace with Hitler. However, Churchill stood firm and chose to continue fighting despite the overwhelming odds. His steadfast refusal to surrender altered the course of history, enabling Britain's survival and paving the way for the Allied counter-offensive that ultimately defeated Hitler.

Intricate and complex problems require relativistic insight - an understanding we must seek through prayer. Recognizing that good judgment or the best course of action can differ depending on one's perspective, we must have faith in embracing diverse viewpoints. This openness provides us with the crucial advantage needed to navigate and overcome our challenges.

Blockchain

Based on my global and extensive experience with banks and financial institutions, I've found that while their business models are essential to the functioning of modern economies, they are fundamentally flawed - propped up by legal frameworks so complex they often become traps that few truly understand. We need to strongly resist 'complexity' in financial institutions and some of the legal minds who focus on entrapment, not grace.

Much has already been said and written by others about the dysfunction of our financial systems - it is sufficient only to note that blockchain has offered a much-needed breathing space and introduced the kind of competition that traditional banks have long resisted.

'Blockchain' is a digital ledger technology that underpins Bitcoin and other cryptocurrencies - an open, decentralized, and distributed system that securely records information, such as financial transactions, in a verifiable manner across a publicly accessible network. In this section, my focus is on blockchain technology itself, not on Bitcoin.

Blockchain substantially reduces the 'complexities' found in traditional legal documents, which technology should be embraced and celebrated, not vilified. Why did the smartphone start feeling like the villain? Because whenever it tried to connect, people accused it of stealing their attention instead of marvelling at the wonder right in their hands! Sometimes, the most valuable things end up getting the most criticism. Here are two examples of how blockchain can simplify the complexities typically found in traditional legal documents:

o   Blockchain establishes a secure, unchangeable record of agreements and transactions that cannot be modified once recorded. This immutability ensures that legal documents, such as contracts or loan agreements, are protected from tampering or version discrepancies.

o   Smart contracts, encoded on the blockchain, can automatically execute and enforce themselves once predefined conditions are satisfied - handling tasks like payments, compliance verification, or contingencies.

Let's be clear: blockchain is an impressive technology and especially valuable for those frustrated with traditional banking systems. However - and this is an important 'however' - it cannot match the elegance and delicacy when grace is sowed into financial transactions or legal documents. 'Grace' is in a league of its own, and I say this with full confidence in my understanding.

My frustration with banks turned into hope when I witnessed several banks in Switzerland and Britain incorporate 'grace' into their transactions (I can't speak for banks in other countries with whom my clients and I have not conducted transactions, so there are undoubtedly some more banks that fall into this category), and especially when I personally observed Capitec Bank and Nedbank in South Africa making genuine efforts to extend grace to their clients.

Business Plans

As a Group, we have initiated a sponsored Business Academy since 2003. One of the stated goals of the Academy is to guide students in preparing profitable and measured Business Plans. Upon reviewing over 1600 business plans, I have never seen 'trust in God, faith, or prayer' incorporated in any of the plans. That said, when I prepared my first business plan, I also made the same grave omission.

How is God honored in our business affairs if we forget about Him? It's a terribly sad omission, and we need to repent for this oversight because hereby we are in effect saying, "I can do this thing alone." Not necessary to elaborate further, suffice only to say "burn the old business plan and start again."

Interestingly, Revelation 3:20 gives us this wonderful invitation: "Behold, I stand at the door and knock. If anyone hears My voice and opens the door, I will come in to him and dine with him, and he with Me." This invitation is not only an invitation to the door of your soul, but it applies to all of life, including an invitation to dwell in your business.

Open wide the doors of your soul and your business affairs, give Jesus the keys of your heart and business, then the Holy Spirit will bring the peace which you may not have, and the provision you so desperately seek.

Simon of Cyrene

In the biblical account in the four Gospels, Simon of Cyrene is a somewhat overlooked individual who was the man compelled by Roman soldiers to help Jesus carry His cross on the way to the crucifixion. Jesus said to His disciples as recorded in Matthew 16:24, "If anyone desires to come after Me, let him deny himself, and take up his cross, and follow Me."

The Bible clearly tells us that you will at some point be carrying your own cross, and your fellow Christian will have the same fate. The point I am making is that there will be situations in your career where someone must help you carry your cross; you will not be able to carry it on your own. The Simon account is to teach Christians that they are to live their lives as one interconnected body, the Church, and we are not to work in the marketplace as lone rangers.

You need to be ready to help carry the cross of another, even when it's not 'your job,' offering the necessary help without requiring a medal for doing so. This act builds trust and loyalty, the seed of great business relationships. Forgiving someone who has hurt you, is an act of reconciliation instead of retaliation after being wronged. This a parallel with the Simon account, by taking on the emotional labor of healing and peace which is often harder than carrying physical weight, yet just as redemptive.

A personal testimony I wish to share. At the time, the church we were attending faced a significant financial challenge - a building project that required more funds than the congregation, already giving generously, could bear. It felt like a cross too heavy for them to carry. In prayer, I sensed a clear prompting in my spirit that I was being called to step in, much like Simon of Cyrene. Initially, I struggled with the idea because Proverbs 11:5 warns, *"He who is surety for a stranger will suffer,"* so this seemed to conflict with the inner prompting I felt. Then, a realization dawned on me - it wasn't foolishness after all. Everything I had belonged to God, so I wasn't standing surety for a stranger, but simply releasing what was already His. I took the step of faith (and my father also wanted to participate), and the outcome was extraordinary. The church completed its building project successfully, and I was deeply blessed in return. My personal experience in intervening was, in a sense, a 'call,' it would be unwise to act in a similar manner if done in presumption or under pressure.

Now, with this Cyrene seed, you can sow on your own prayer altar when your moment arrives and you have need of a friend who can help you carry your own cross. Again, I say, we cannot use methodologies when it comes to Kingdom matters, but we can rely on Galatians 6:7 promise, "for whatever a man sows, that he will also reap."

Word of Knowledge

1 Corinthians 12:8 implicitly states: "for to one is given the word of wisdom through the Spirit, to another the word of knowledge through the same Spirit." Theology sometimes tries to obscure an inclusion in the Word, since some theologians try to argue away (as not being relevant for our time) the gift of a word of knowledge.

This gift is closely related to another gift, the word of wisdom. Both gifts overlap in meaning; they are different facets of information revealed by the Holy Spirit.

I concur with this definition provided from online research on the 'Word of Knowledge': "the supernatural ability to identify, recognize, recall, and restate information, identities, purposes, names, numbers, dates/times, events, places, and pictorial images. This information is revealed by the Holy Spirit instead of originating from man or being uncovered through research."

My father once gave me very valuable instruction: "Alan, when you are in a delicate situation, pause and pray in that very situation for God to guide you." My father did not specifically refer to a 'word of knowledge,' but that is what he was referring to.

The inference here is that business individuals should, when placed in very delicate situations, seek the guidance of the Holy Spirit in the form of a 'word of knowledge' or a 'word of wisdom.' This is not your standard morning prayer; this prayer needs to be a specific request for the Holy Spirit to gift you with a 'word of knowledge' for this [name-specific] situation. This request must stem from a sincere heart, without selfish gain.

I have personally experienced many instances where I have asked for a 'word of knowledge' in delicate situations and received the gift. Here is one such case:

I was asked by a pastoral friend to meet with his friend, who was seeking some Christian discipleship. After meeting with the individual on several occasions, he wanted to introduce me to his wider family, not knowing that he was the cousin of a King of an important region. When I arrived at the city to meet his cousin (the King), I was picked up from my Hotel by an entourage of people who took me to the King. While travelling by car for several hours, I had a witness in my Spirit that I needed to lay hands on the King as "a servant of the Lord." My first response was to ask for a restroom break (so I could hopefully find a space to hide). Take note that at this point, I did not know whether the King was even a 'Christian,' and now I (as a stranger) must be so bold as to lay hands on him.

When I met the King and had lunch with him and his wider family, I so hoped that feeling I had would have passed by now. It did not, and I felt increasingly nauseous. I then remembered my father's counsel to pray for a 'word of knowledge.' I silently prayed while munching on something (at that time, I would just munch on anything) and received a word of knowledge. I cautiously proceeded to ask the King whether he knew why "he became King" since he was not the first in line (as I was told). He said, "he was unsure," to which I replied, "Sir, it's because your mother prayed for you."

Let's pause a moment here. Some readers would presume this was good guesswork, as it's quite common to say, "Your mother prayed for you." Well, remember I did not know whether anyone in his family was Christian; it could also possibly be that the father was Christian and the mother was not. Anyway, the point is that I received the 'word of knowledge' as given and resisted the temptation of figuring it out.

The King immediately caught on that 'this was some special knowledge' to which he replied that he was a reborn Christian, and that it was true that his mother did pray for him and "by the way" he said, "my mother happens to be visiting and she is in the other room." His mother was asked to come out, we hugged each other as we greeted, and I proceeded to lay hands on the King (now that the Holy Spirit gave me credibility in front of the King) with his praying mother as a witness.

Word of Wisdom

Closely related to the word of knowledge (which I specifically requested in prayer in the previous example) is a word of wisdom, which in my case was gifted to me without my specific request (this is just how it happened to me, I am not making a theological deduction).

We need to be expectant of both words of wisdom and knowledge in our marketplace dealings; do not suppress or forget about these two gifts. A true case example:

I was once caught by surprise in a corporate court attack by a skillful and shrewd litigant, with only days to appear in court. My existing legal counsel at the time was not available since they had another case in hand, so I decided to appear in court myself without counsel (yes, I could have asked for a time extension, but I did not). While waiting outside the court, hoping that I had all my case evidence procedurally correct, a 'word of wisdom' dropped in my spirit that "I was not to speak until the Judge invites me." The Judge never invited me to speak, I said nothing, allowing the opposition to rattle on until they caught themselves in their own web of falsehoods – I won my case without uttering a word.

My younger son made only two requests of me when I set out to write this book. The first, which I have already recounted, concerned my very costly decision on the Swiss Board. The second arose from a word of wisdom imparted to me during another precarious episode. At the time, I was serving as Chairman of a company that faced a capitalisation shortfall. Summoned by a Chieftain to answer for this failing, I was sternly reprimanded. In that tense moment, the word of wisdom I received was simple yet profound: 'Call our accountant while still in the person's presence' (these are not the exact words, for words of wisdom are impressions left upon the heart). I did so, and our accountant informed me that he had been trying to reach me with exciting news—the British Pound had strengthened significantly against the Swiss Franc that very day. Since the Company accounts were denominated in Swiss Francs but reserves held in British Pounds, the supposed shortfall had, in fact, vanished.

One of Aesop's fables (ancient and famous moral tales attributed to Aesop, a storyteller from Greece) is that of the 'Sparrow and the Peacock':

> One day, a humble Sparrow flew into the royal gardens of the Great Peacock King. The palace shimmered with gold and jewels, and peacocks with glorious tails strutted through the marble courtyards.
>
> The Sparrow, plain and dusty from travel, landed near a fountain and admired the beauty all around. "Who are you to come before the Peacock King?" sneered a young peacock. "You have no color, no grace, no elegance."
>
> The Sparrow bowed her head. "I bring no beauty, but I bring news. A storm is coming from the east, swift and strong. I thought the King should know."
>
> The peacocks laughed. "What does a storm matter to us? We are under the King's protection."

But the Sparrow was granted an audience with the King. Quiet and regal, the Peacock King listened, then nodded. "Thank you, little one," he said. "We shall take shelter."

When the storm struck with fury, only the Sparrow and those who heeded her were safe.

True to life, as exemplified in this fable, is that wisdom, not wealth or display, brings honor in the presence of power.

The Sacrament of Communion

A sacrament is a symbol of a spiritual reality. One of the Bible verses that records the institution of the Lord's Supper (Holy Communion) is in 1 Corinthians 11:24-25.

"And when [Jesus] had given thanks, He broke [the bread] and said, "Take, eat; this is My body which is broken for you; do this in remembrance of Me." In the same manner, [Jesus] also took the cup after supper, saying, "This cup is the new covenant in My blood. This do, as often as you drink it, in remembrance of Me."

While our memories well preserve a poisonous weed, we quickly forget the enormous sacrifice and complete victory of Calvary. As forgetfulness is a lamentable fact, Jesus rather encourages us to break the bread of communion "in remembrance of Me."

Jesus, our Lord, where we would think that our memory would linger, is sadly swiftly surpassed by some business matter which steals away our heart. This distractedness is addressed by Jesus' encouragement to drink from the cup of His blood as a sacrament of the new covenant of grace.

Why do I introduce the sacrament of communion in a marketplace setting? Simply because it helps us to remain focused on Jesus in the volatile Game of Thrones, and will be a reminder not to permit our hearts to be stolen by our business affairs. I daily take communion both for my personal and business affairs, and it makes a significant difference. There is no overstating the profound importance of taking communion "in remembrance of Him."

Submission

At a vulnerable time of a deep and painful trial, I was gently woken up in the early morning hours by the Holy Spirit with the words 'submit.' My prayer was to win and see victory, but 'submission' was a curveball reply to my prayer. Let's be guided by the Bible in this regard:

Job 22:21 says something interesting – "Now acquaint yourself with Him, and be at peace; Thereby, good will come to you."

1 Peter 5:5 adds to Job – "Likewise, you younger people, submit yourselves to your elders. Yes, all of you be submissive to one another, and be clothed with humility."

The goal of submission is given in 1 Peter 5:6 – "Therefore humble yourselves under the mighty hand of God, that He may exalt you in due time, casting all your care upon Him, for He cares for you."

We extract from this important clues for living a victorious life, namely: (i) acquaint ourselves with God, (ii) when we are growing in our Christian walk, submit to our elders in the Lord, (iii) all have an attitude of submission to one another, (iv) steps one to three are the stairsteps to submission before God so that God's promise can be fulfilled to "exalt us in due time" (because He cares for us).

The great discovery I made in my victory over adversity is that we do not need an Einstein code to unlock ourselves; we need to be guided by the light of Scripture, where 'submission to God' plays a pivotal role. Submission unlocks the burden of trying to control everything and frees us from the mental strain of going it alone.

Submission, repentance, and forgiveness form a sort of trio. When critics challenge you by asking, "What makes you so special that you can forgive others? Do you think you don't need forgiveness yourself?" A proper response is this: "In the Lord's

Prayer, Jesus taught us to first ask for forgiveness for our own trespasses before we forgive those who trespass against us. This shows that true forgiveness begins with repentance. Therefore, forgiving others is not a claim to moral superiority, but rather an act of submission to God and one that flows from recognizing our own need for grace."

Another one of Aesop's fables is that of "The Oak and the Reeds." The summary of the fable is a strong oak that mocks the reeds for bending in the wind. When a storm comes, the oak is uprooted, but the reeds survive because they bend with the wind. The moral being that submission surpasses strength.

The Seven Spirits of God

As we grow in maturity along our business journey, we've come to realize the importance of decoding the mysteries of God's revelation to us. This revelation comes in many forms - words of wisdom and knowledge, asymmetrical insights for decision-making, fresh perspectives on mathematics, and more. However, our main objective is not just to gather these individual revelations and attempt to piece them together, but to begin operating under the Spirit of Revelation itself.

Revelation 5:6 gives us a brief snippet into the Spirit of Revelation: "Then I saw a Lamb [Jesus Christ], looking as if it had been slain, standing at the center of the throne, encircled by the four living creatures and the elders. The Lamb had seven horns and seven eyes, which are the seven spirits of God sent out into all the earth." The seven Spirits of God are not seven distinct spirits, but rather seven manifestations of the Holy Spirit, representing the fullness of the Holy Spirit's power and influence, often linked to the attributes described in Isaiah 11:2 –"The Spirit of the Lord will rest on him - the Spirit of wisdom and of understanding, the Spirit of counsel and of might, the Spirit of the knowledge and fear of the Lord."

What then are the seven manifestations of the Holy Spirit? They are the Spirit of the Lord, the Spirit of Wisdom, the Spirit of Understanding, the Spirit of Counsel, the Spirit of Might, the Spirit of Knowledge, and the Spirit of the Fear of the Lord. It is imperative we briefly consider the attributes of each Spirit:

o   The Spirit of the Lord is the Spirit of Power, and it is through Him that we receive God's power.

o   The Spirit of Wisdom empowers us to make sound decisions. It grants us the ability to grasp complex ideas and apply them in ways that bring benefit to ourselves and those around us.

o   The Spirit of Understanding, which also empowers us to make sound decisions, operates in practical ways in our lives. It enhances our relationships by helping us discern the reasons behind people's actions. With that insight, we're able to respond with compassion instead of anger, becoming instruments of peace in challenging situations.

- The Spirit of Counsel serves as our helper, guiding us in alignment with God's will for our lives. As our Counsellor, the Holy Spirit reveals what is right and wrong, and directs us on what to pursue or to avoid.

- The Spirit of Might empowers Spirit-filled believers to endure life's trials and overcome each new challenge. It is through this attribute of the Holy Spirit that we are equipped to fulfil God's will for our lives.

- The Spirit of Knowledge goes beyond mere information or facts - it's an intimate, transformative experience that often comes through revelation or deep insight. It is the kind of understanding that shapes us when we grasp mysteries in truth on a profound level.

- The Spirit of Fear of the Lord is the reverence, respect, and heart revelation of the Sovereignty of God.

Understanding the Seven Spirits of God is essential, as it reveals Jesus' perfect unity with the Holy Spirit from the very beginning of time. This divine partnership empowers His mission and shapes His judgment. The Seven Spirits also bridge the revelations of the Old and New Testaments, showing how God's Spirit has been consistently at work, fulfilling prophecy.

In the context of the marketplace, the manifestations of the Seven Spirits of God remind us that the Spirit operates through power, wisdom, and understanding, and counsel, fear of the Lord, knowledge, and might, not just through miraculous signs. Most businesspeople focus solely on seeking miracles, which narrows their perspective, often causes them to overlook the voice of the Spirit, Who moves and manifests in a variety of ways.

God's Sovereignty

Corrie ten Boom, a Christian watchmaker, was arrested with her sister (Betsie) by the Nazis during World War II (because they hid Jews in their home) and sent to a brutal concentration camp for women. Corrie and her sister experienced incomprehensible suffering in the camp, yet despite this pain, a miraculous event happened.

Corrie and Betsie held secret Bible studies and prayer meetings with other prisoners, a seed of unexpected hope for the other prisoners. One day, Corrie was complaining about the fleas in their barracks, which evaded everything. Betsie reminded Corrie of God's sovereignty and that Corrie should change her attitude to one of thanks in all circumstances. Corrie had a hard time feeling grateful for fleas, but later they discovered that the guards avoided their barracks because of the fleas, which allowed them to hold Bible studies without interruption.

Charles Spurgeon aptly states, "Fewer doctrines of the Christian faith are more comforting than the sovereignty of God. It humbles you in good seasons, provides hope in hard seasons, and gives joy in all seasons. The doctrine of God's sovereignty is a constant nourishment for the soul."

The prolific literary evangelist, A.W. Pink, says, "The sovereignty of God may be defined as the exercise of His supremacy. Being infinitely elevated above the highest creature, He is the Most High, Lord of heaven and earth. Subject to none, influenced by none, absolutely independent; God does as He pleases, only as He pleases."

God's sovereign control ensures that everything unfolds according to His purpose and design. This signifies that we experience His control and authority in every aspect of life, making it impossible to escape either His justice or His love. God's sovereign lordship is not limited to His control; it also includes His authority - His right to be obeyed. In the covenant Moses brings to Israel following their deliverance from Egypt by God's sovereign hand, God begins by declaring Himself as Lord (Exodus 20:1–2). On the foundation of this declaration, God then delivers the Ten Commandments.

This divine doctrine needs to be studied studiously, reflected on constantly, meditated upon, and breathed into our souls. In the night of adversity, as paraphrased from Charles Spurgeon, "God's sovereignty is the pillow on which we lay our heads in peace."

Symbolism of Imagery - Decoding

By now, you are probably wondering about the meaning behind the images featuring the soldier at the start of each chapter? Much of the imagery is straightforward, but here are the more subtle details decoded (to my female readers: while I've used the masculine form here, the message always applies equally to you. The imagery simply reflects a single character for illustrative purposes) -

o The images in Chapters 2 and 3 depict a businessperson in the early stages of his career - unaware of the risks, learning many skills, and beginning to carve out his professional path.

o The image in Chapter 4 reflects coded arrows being crafted around the clock, unnoticed by the businessperson. Notably, the 'king's chair' is absent in the first three images. The grass is green and the sky is blue, very rosy indeed!

o The 'king's chair' suddenly appears in the Chapter 5 image, symbolizing the moment the businessperson sets his sights on a clear goal and begins moving forward with determination. Now the trouble begins, but the Word of God (Ephesians 6:10-18) has taught the soldier to "be strong in the Lord and in the power of His might. Put on the whole armor of God, that you may be able to stand against the wiles of the devil." Following the guidance of Scripture, the soldier in the image wisely puts on the 'whole armor of God' illustrated by (i) the belt of truth; (ii) the breastplate of righteousness; (iii) the shoes of the Gospel of peace; (iv) the shield of faith; (v) the helmet of salvation; and (vi) the sword of the Spirit. The soldier consistently wears a formal business tie as a symbolic gesture of his prayerful regard for the marketplace.

- The image in Chapter 6 captures the soldier's exhaustion and confusion, overwhelmed by the intensity of conflict in the marketplace. In the thick of his troubles, he fails to wear parts of his armor, despite Scripture's call to "put on the whole armor of God."

- In a mysterious turn, the soldier regains his strength as reflected in the Chapter 7 image, witnessing flowers bloom once more through the rain brought by the Lord to his situation. In my case, the Protea flowers symbolized the world-class education that the Lord reminded me that shaped my thinking: first through Grey College and the University of KwaZulu-Natal in South Africa, and later (as symbolized by the Roses) through the exceptional schooling my children received at The Croft School and Warwick School in England, and at Stellenbosch University in South Africa. At this stage of his journey, the soldier begins to sense that something deeper is unfolding, and he now views the 'king's chair' with new eyes.

- The image in Chapter 8 shows that the soldier had experienced a heart transformation. His career is no longer his top priority; instead, we see him on his knees, constructing something entirely different. The soldier understands God's whisper for the marketplace - extending and teaching grace as the priority, building bridges, and aligning with Matthew 6:33 – "But seek ye first the kingdom of God, and his righteousness; and all these things shall be added unto you." Sequencing in God's order is seen here, namely: first apply His Word, then thereafter, experience His grace.

o   Now that the business bridge is complete, the soldier begins to behold the stars of the universe as displayed by the Chapter 9 image - symbolizing divine wisdom and a new, higher way to advance his career.

Decoding Beyond Formulas

Decoding the marketplace isn't just about formulas or strategies. It's about learning to see through God's written Word, to recognize His work in your life in places most people overlook. Whether we've talked about faith multiplying our efforts or the value of seeking a word of knowledge in a tough moment, the heart of it all is this: God is involved in every part of your life, including your business life.

The marketplace is God's creation. The Holy Spirit walks with you through contracts, setbacks, late nights, and tough decisions. The spiritual gifts and principles we've explored aren't meant to stay in devotionals, neither are they complete as nobody can comprehend the breadth, length, depth, or height of God's work. Discussion should also be made of the Courts of Heaven, which has been extensively explored by insightful authors who have provided valuable perspectives on the subject.

Spiritual gifts and principles belong right where you work, where you plan, where you lead. God's voice doesn't just speak in quiet rooms. He speaks in busy offices, tense meetings, and moments of financial pressure.

You might feel unqualified or unsure of how to move forward with all of this. That's okay. The goal is not to master a perfect method, but to grow in relationship with the One who gives wisdom freely when we ask.

You were not meant to navigate all this alone. And you don't have to figure everything out before you begin. What matters most is staying close to God, inviting Him into the process, and trusting that even when the path seems unclear, He is still guiding your steps.

So, keep going. Keep asking questions. Keep praying bold prayers. Don't just look at your bank account and call it reality. Let faith reshape your understanding of what's possible. God can do more with your small, surrendered "yes" than all the effort in the world without Him.

You are not just a businessperson. You are a carrier of divine wisdom. You are not just solving problems. You are building something which will be of use to you and your fellow pilgrims on this journey. Walk forward with peace, not pressure. Let God be the foundation you build on. The world doesn't need more brilliance; it needs more people who are applying God's Word to everyday life. And if you do that, you won't just decode the mystery but also start becoming the answer.

CHAPTER 10
STEPPING INTO DESTINY

"Christ in you, the hope of glory."

(Colossians 1:27)

Socrates used to say, "Philosophers can be happy without music," but Christians can be happier than philosophers when all outward supports or treasures are withdrawn. That's because it's always been Christ in me, the hope of glory. Mary and Martha were favored with occasional visits from Jesus, but with the new Covenant, it's not mere occasional visits, because now He has formed in me the hope of glory.

No promise of God is only of private interpretation; the promises found in the Bible are applicable to all believers in a Triune God (Father, Son, and Holy Spirit). Christians often forget that no extraordinary promise from God is beyond their reach, and no grace is too vast for them. There is no well of living water from which you are excluded from drinking.

We all know that God has repeatedly said that He will never leave or forsake us. The Word of God extends wisdom to us to deal with the Game of Thrones in the marketplace, and to succeed in the Game with God as your Partner. How can I say this so boldly? Well, simply because there is nothing in heaven or on earth which is not contained in God's promise that "He will never leave or forsake us." Let's not complicate a very straightforward promise.

The God of Jacob

Business participants too often feel dirty and worthless in the mudslinging Game of Thrones. This is one of the reasons that we may only feel energetic or 'clean' one day a week to attend church or pray one or two times a week – the rest of the time, we need to 'clean' ourselves of the worries and dirt hurled at us.

The following revelation, brought by a few theologians on the subject, will be helpful to you concerning your 'inherent worth,' despite how you look in the mirror. As a first step you need to restore your spiritual dignity, which should best be found in Jesus' finished work on the cross for you, but individuals struggle to conceptualize this so it will be most helpful to understand why God identifies Himself in many places in the Bible as the "God of Abraham, Isaac, and Jacob."

This name of God signifies the covenant God made with Israel. Jacob was the grandson of patriarch Abraham and the son of Isaac. I will not cover the history of Abraham and Isaac, but God's referencing the name 'Jacob' and not his new name 'Israel' is important to understand.

Unlike his father and grandfather, Jacob was not a role model. In fact, he was a swindler, a liar, and even stole the birthright from his brother Esau. It's only after God changed his name from 'Jacob' to 'Israel' did Jacob's character improve, this after Jacob's infamous wrestling match with God recorded in Genesis 32.

Jacob is also a fearful man, often paired with the word 'fear,' and despite Jacob's numerous failings, we see God identifying himself as the 'God of Jacob,' as opposed to the 'God of [Jacob's improved character name] Israel.' In this, we learn that God is not swayed by our failings or weaknesses; rather, we find that in those weaknesses, God is strong on our behalf.

Christians in the marketplace must comprehend that Jacob's victory and change of name were not the result of his own strength and effort but came through desperate weakness. Jacob clung to God until blessing was acquired, and please read this carefully: despite his many failings God honored Jacob (i) with a new name and most (x2) remarkably (ii) the name 'Jacob' lost was borne by God as part of His own name and hereby to identify Himself with us. Be encouraged hereby that God is concerned with the burdened, the lost, and the fearful.

No-Lose Methodology

The no-lose problem-solving methodology is based on recognized philosophy in conflict situations, which simply aims to meet the needs of both conflicting parties. Different methods are used for this problem-solving, but broadly, the methods apply the principles of equality, empathy, and active listening.

In 2017, I had a spiritual encounter of a type of download of a similar method for Government economies. The principles and models to be applied are relatively straightforward, and as a student who majored in Economics, I know that these insights will reap great gains for Government coffers, individuals, and companies alike (if applied). Will AI provide a comparatively competitive solution? No, because AI is data-driven. By 'no-lose' applied here, I mean not a perfect 'no-lose' but rather for the coffers of Governments and individuals/businesses to escalate simultaneously within low-risk parameters.

I was more bewildered than anyone as to why I received these insights, but this can only be as 1 Corinthians 1:27 records: "But God has chosen the foolish things of the world to put to shame the wise, and God has chosen the weak things of the world to put to shame the things which are mighty."

Governments cannot be Christian; they can only profess a broad-based acknowledgement of Christian values. Only individuals can choose to be Christian, and this book's stated goal is for you, as an individual, to comprehend that it is all about "Christ in you, the hope of glory." Harmful codes cannot destroy you, cannot take away your hope, and cannot destroy your future (if you submit to God's guidance in your life).

This book is intended as an aid in the problem-solving of marketplace participants, which, to my deep surprise, is more complex than the solutions for the economic prosperity of governments. Maybe that is correct, because when we talk about individuals (as opposed to Government systems), we speak about individuals made in the image of God.

Let's now move forward to decoding solutions to mental health, dignity, and wealth, which is to go and wash yourself in the River of Grace and do it several times, just as Namaan was instructed by God's servant, the Prophet Elisha.

Herein lies the revelation: Solutions to difficult problems, discovered God's way, rest in its simplicity, not in its complexity. Below are guidelines, which are not exhaustive, but rest on the principle of 'simplicity.'

Destiny

There is the true story of an evangelist with large ministry debts who once heard God tell him to buy an abandoned factory for $280,000. He approached the realtor, offered him the price, and was laughed out of the realtor's office. He knew the price offered was incredibly low because the building was worth substantially more, but he obeyed God's direction. Within weeks, the anxious seller accepted the offer, to the surprise of the realtor and the evangelist.

Being the head of a large ministry that did church plants, the evangelist did what came naturally and started a church in the new building. It just made sense. Then he believed God chastised him, "I didn't tell you to put a church in that building. You failed to listen to me." The evangelist realized he had started right, but began to finish God's sentences, without ever asking Him for direction. He moved the church out of the building and waited on God, who then directed, "Sell the building. List it for $1.6 million." Within weeks, the building sold for the asking price, and the evangelist was able to use the profits to repay all his ministry debts, and God was able to open new doors of destiny that he had never even imagined.

The story of the biblical Abraham gives us clues to the foundational principles that apply to the victorious future of all Christians:

(i)   First, God births a vision in us, but

(ii)   when that vision is delayed, we

(iii) may attempt to fulfil that vision through our efforts, which

(iv)   leads to abject failure to fulfil the vision, resulting in

(v)   the death of the vision. Suddenly,

(vi) after passing through the door of adversity,

(vii) the vision is supernaturally reborn, then

(viii) out of our utter dependence on God comes the miraculous fulfilment of the vision,

(ix) bringing a breakthrough to destiny.

For this reason, I believe that there are five D's associated with Matthew 5:3 – "Blessed are the poor in spirit, for theirs is the kingdom of heaven:"

o First, *Destitution* when everything falls apart; then

o *Detachment* from self as you try to fix the problem, but nothing works, leading to

o *Disclosure* or repentance of all known sins (out of desperation); resulting in

o *Declaration* of thanksgiving for the circumstances you are experiencing because it's God's will, next

o *Dependence* on God when He starts to work supernaturally in one's life.[166]

Everywhere we look in the Bible we see this same amazing pattern, the death of a dream that we know is God-inspired, before we finally die to our own efforts to bring it to pass, and allow Him to resurrect not only the dream, but the destiny it births, to the glory of God.

We have discovered that circumstances lead us to the Valley of Adversity, then this Valley flows to the Sea of Grace, all this traversing because of this: we need to fear God and impart grace. But why? Because the inheritance is ahead of us as promised by Proverbs 21:21 - "he who follows righteousness and mercy [grace] finds life, righteousness and honor." Proverbs 22:4 goes further: "By humility [grace] and the fear of the Lord are riches and honor and life."

Freedom

I have walked around large parts of the globe in my marketplace shoes and many extra miles that most people never have to walk. I have experienced darkness and a sense of helplessness, but I have come out of that dark valley, with God's grace, to properly decode the circumstances.

I believe that my unique life experience has prepared and taught me some invaluable lessons over nearly four decades, most from the *University of Adversity*. Over the years, I have been confronted by bullies more times than I can count and insulted more often than I have shouted, "Jack Sparrow!" I have frequently been misunderstood and falsely accused, often betrayed, endured many painful years of insomnia (sleeping only three to four hours a night), experienced a debilitating back injury from my years in sport, as well as theft and deception.

271

On the flip side, I have enjoyed the heights of business success and healthy family relationships [I was schooled to relay a testimony of personal successes down to a few words only].

Probably just like you, I often struggle with these devilish codes and the Lord's command to love my enemies. At times when I wake up, I drag myself to the prayer closet, knowing that I must mentally prepare for another day of commercial onslaught and the nonsense that many people in commerce often communicate. Also, a great challenge is daily facing selfish interests and dealing with those who have no fear of God or extend no grace to mankind.

I have earned my stripes in the battlefield, and it's these wounds and life experiences which have helped me to decode marketplace experiences. A significant lesson I learnt: Your smile draws people in, but it's your wounds that create a true connection. Be encouraged, dear reader, from the promise God made in Isaiah 61:1, which you will experience:

"The Lord is today preaching good tidings to the poor; He is healing the financially brokenhearted, He is now proclaiming liberty to the captives, He is now opening the prison doors to those who are bound."

I am fully persuaded that God wants us to enjoy financial freedom and to be free from the harmful codes and practices that bind so many people today.

In Roman times, if an individual owed money he/she was thrown in jail and a list of the debts owed was nailed on the door of his/her cell. Only when the debt was settled was the prisoner released, but of course, there was nothing the prisoner could do to redeem the debt because he/she was stuck in the cell. It is also a picture of our helplessness in the face of the debt of sin we owe to God, with the only way to pay it being death - hence the love of God in sending Christ and nailing all our sin debts to the Cross.[167]

Modern-Day Slavery

The reality is that people want to be free of financial slavery more than just about anything else they desire. By way of illustration, I think we can agree that any US President Trump have the X Factor and know how to pull in a crowd.

So, imagine an occasion where the US President is scheduled to give a major speech at a large convention center. No doubt the event would be a sell-out. They arrive on a beautiful summers evening with crowds lining the streets. Security is tight, and the crowds are excited as they make their way to the event.

Mr. Bridges, a wealthy individual, has also scheduled his conference at the building adjacent to the same convention center. He arrives in a taxi with a few banners under his arm, with no helpers. As people hurry by, Mr. Bridges starts placing his banners at strategic points along the way in full view of the standing crowds, which simply read:

"Bank Guaranteed, Interest-Free Loans to All Applicants – Tonight Only"

I am quietly confident that there would be plenty of empty seats at the US President's event, such is the XX factor *power of money*. All the star power in the world would be easily diffused, and their crowd diverted by those ten simple words! Perhaps more importantly, the response of the people in this story is a clear indication of people's desperate desire to be free from financial debt and the slavery it brings.

Slavery is a curse that has dogged humanity for millennia. It is the ultimate degradation of the human spirit, a fundamental declaration that slaves have no inherent value as human beings. Slaves have never been valued for who they are, only for what they can do. From the time of Roman law, they were classified not as people, but as possessions, which meant they had no rights whatsoever.

Remarkably, as recently as 1857, the United States Supreme Court ruled in the case of *Dred Scott vs. Stanford* that Mr. Scott's application to be freed from slavery could not be granted because African Americans were not citizens and therefore had no right to sue in Federal Court. This case has been cited as one of the catalysts that precipitated the American Civil War, which in turn reflects the level of force often necessary to free people from the bondage of slavery.

The truth is that there is something deep in the soul of every man and woman that instinctively realizes they are intended to live in freedom, not in slavery. To this day, in many countries, slavery still exists, where people are literally deprived of freedom against their will and forced to serve the will of others — undoubtedly, the worst form of slavery is sex trafficking.

Yet the reality is that a more subtle form of slavery stalks us all because we can become enslaved by whatever we choose to serve. The most pervasive form is financial slavery, when we make money and the pursuit of riches our god, in the hope that when we make enough, we will have the freedom to do whatever we want.

Interestingly, Jesus spoke frequently about the deceitfulness of riches, not because money is inherently bad, but because He knew the power it has to enslave people and to distract them from the true riches of a grace relationship with God. In Matthew 6:24, Jesus said: "No one can serve two masters; for either he will hate the one and love the other, or else he will be loyal to the one and despise the other. You cannot serve God and mammon."

It is also important to note that it is not the amount of money that enslaves; it is the fact that its hold is sufficient to keep you on a treadmill that you seemingly cannot escape. The person who has a credit card debt of say $5,000 because they bought things they could not afford and did not need to impress people they did not know is just as bound as the businessman who over-extended himself by buying machinery that is financed to the hilt by the bank.

The power of money and its hold is so great that the only answer and the only antidote is God. People are lured into the deception that the person with money is the one who wields the power and makes the rules. And while it's true that those who are in debt are, in a sense, captive to those they owe, the truth is that the greatest power lies with God and God alone.

In a lesson that cost me millions, I learned the hard way that you cannot beat mammon with any amount of money, ability, or education. The only time I found victory was through adversity and the revelation that God has a different, albeit paradoxical way, to fulfil my dreams, and yours too. Here are three steps that will guide you on your path to freedom:

Humble yourself: The first thing to do is to humble yourself and to recognize that you are in a place of captivity, and stop singing, "I owe, I owe, so off to work I go," as the bills keep piling up.

Recognize who you are: Next, recognize that you are where you are because of the choices you have made.

Make right decisions: Then make the right decision to turn your back on the god of mammon (that is, toward indebtedness) and your face toward the living God, who promises to supply all your needs according to His riches in glory by Christ Jesus. He knows what you need, and He will faithfully provide for you as you follow Him.

Failing Forward

You may think you are in the darkest jail of debt or the sticky web of all these codes, with no way forward and no way out, but God always has the last word, and the Bible clearly directs that *there is no trial from which God cannot provide a way of escape.*

You may believe that you have failed and are trapped, but you need to remember that failure is an event, not a person. Well-known author and speaker John Maxwell coined the phrase 'failing forward,' which simply implies learning from our mistakes to continue moving forward.

I agree with John Maxwell that there is one differentiating factor that separates those who consistently shine from those who don't: "The difference between average people and achieving people is their perception of and response to failure."[168] J. Wallace Hamilton goes further and states, "The increase of suicides, alcoholics, and even some forms of nervous breakdowns is evidence that many people are training for success when they should be training for failure. Failure is far more common than success; poverty is more prevalent than wealth; and disappointment is more normal than arrival."[169]

John Maxwell[170] offers wise advice regarding what not to do with failure (failing backward) versus the wise approach (failing forward) amongst others such as (i) blaming others (failing backward) v taking responsibility (failing forward); or (ii) quitting work (failing backward) v persevering (failing forward); or (iii) repeating the same mistakes (failing backward) v learning from each mistake (failing forward), etc.

So much of our success or failure is dictated by how we process things mentally. Sound biblical truths are often reflected in much of the top motivational teaching available today. "As a man thinks in his heart, so is he." "Attitude determines altitude." The list goes on and on, but in essence, whether we succeed or fail or whether we overcome or are overcome, depends on the choices we make, more specifically, the way we respond to adversity.

Failing Forward Testimonies

The power of perseverance and the value of learning to fall forward are borne out in many testimonies. A remarkable failing forward testimony is that of Louis Braille (my long-lost cousin – I wish), who was born in France in 1809. As a child, while observing his father make shoes, he picked up a sharp, pointed awl, which slipped, pierced his eye, and damaged it beyond repair. The other eye soon became infected, and before long, Louis was completely blind.

At the age of ten, Louis was sent to a school for blind children in Paris, where children were taught to read and write using a system of raised letters. But this system was difficult to use as it was hard to tell the letters apart. One day, a soldier by the name of Charles Barbier visited the school. He had developed a system for reading messages in the dark based upon a series of raised dots. Louis realized the potential for this system and developed it so that it could be used for blind people, the same system that now bears his name and is used in almost every country in the world.

Then there is the remarkable story of Nicholas James Vujicic, a Serbian-Australian evangelist and motivational speaker born with Tetra-Amelia Syndrome, a rare disorder characterized by the absence of all four limbs (arms and legs). He coined and lived the catchphrase: "Attitude is Altitude." Since his first speaking engagement at age nineteen, Nick has traveled around the world, sharing his story with millions, sometimes in stadiums at full capacity. He is also the founder of the highly successful 'Life without Limbs' organization. Today, this dynamic young evangelist has accomplished more than most people achieve in a lifetime.

Finally, on a lighter note, there is the lesson my then-seven-year-old daughter taught my wife and me. One day, her math teacher asked to meet with my wife because Ame was not performing to the high standard of the math curriculum, and they needed to downgrade her to another class. My wife had the difficult task of gently breaking the bad news that Ame was going to be moved to another class because of her weak math skills, to which she replied, "Great, Mom, now I'll be able to understand what the teacher is saying!"

Over the years, I've been fortunate to be exposed to many wise men and women of God, who gave me deep revelatory insight. Such a good friend, Duncan, often shared the following insight with me: "Apply the Testudo."

Apply the Testudo

In ancient Roman warfare, the Roman Legions used what was called a testudo formation in battle, which is the interlocking of shields that create a type of tortoise shell to cover the forward advance of soldiers while at the same time protecting their backs from artillery attack. The forward elements of the formation would bring up their shields to protect their vital areas, while the rearward elements raised their shields up and over the soldier in front of them. This innovative battle formation provided maximum protection from enemy fire because it was so difficult to penetrate.

However, the testudo only works when there is complete unity; if a single person breaks ranks, the strategy is doomed to fail. In the same way that the testudo works to protect advancing armies, family members can lay aside their own devices and use it, by uniting to protect each other, and in the end, to protect and preserve the entire family unit, from the onslaughts of both the devil and the darts hurled by the world. This is exactly the design plan in the heart of God from the beginning of creation, and He longs for it to be restored, to bless those He loves.

When embracing the testudo, remember that in the end, all men are mere humans and subject to change. That makes it even more important for us to cling tightly to God as the heart of the testudo.

A Dealer in Hope

One day, while I was standing emotionally drained at beautiful Lake Zurich in Switzerland, my mind was mulling over all the challenges I was facing, with enormous financial responsibilities and enemies swirling in other countries. It was certainly not a time to be faint-hearted, and to make matters worse, my default position under attack is always to fight back, whilst God was encouraging me to stand still.

That day at Lake Zurich I decided to change my direction and go back to my roots, which meant that I would once again become a child and return to the place where years earlier I prayed a heartfelt prayer for God to help me with an exam paper which I was about to fail - that I miraculously passed with distinction. From that moment on, I would no longer rely on my academic knowledge or my years of commercial experience, and I would completely stop relying on my influential contacts. Lake Zurich is forever etched in my memory as a defining moment.

To conquer my many Goliaths, I would become a dealer in hope. At the turn of the 19th Century, Napoleon Bonaparte defined a leader as a "dealer in hope," but in that case, hope was merely a secular belief in good outcomes for business or military ventures. His concept of hope was to take obstacles and transform them into possibilities. It is important here to realize that optimism is a passive virtue while hope is active. It takes no courage to be an optimist, but it takes a great deal of courage to have hope.

Although Bonaparte's concept of hope sounds good, I had little use for secular notions. I was simply, and like a child, going to apply Hebrews 4:16 to my life: "Let us then approach God's throne of grace with confidence, so that we may receive mercy and find grace to help us in our time of need." My heavenly Father was the Owner and Master of the Universe, so I would go to Him for help.

My hope was based on the expectation that when I approach God's throne of grace in prayer, the King's scepter may be lifted, allowing heaven's gates to open. However, I knew I could only approach God's holy throne with clean hands and a pure heart, so I went to my hotel room and repented over everything I could possibly think of. I even repented for once being very angry at our dog; anything, in order to turn things around.

Later, I purchased a hymn book from which I used to sing as a child in the Anglican Church. I found great comfort singing hymns in my Swiss hotel room while other hotel guests were counting their money in adjacent rooms. I had approached the Throne of Grace many times before in my life, but this time it was different; my life was about to change, and I knew it.

The deep meaning of Hebrews 4:16 became a reality to me. Still, I also wondered whether that tremendous challenge was in preparation for becoming mighty in the Spirit – but then I was struck by the revelation of Zechariah 4:6: "Not by might nor by power, but by My Spirit." There is one stronghold that the church has yet to conquer, and that's the stranglehold of debt and the dominance of Monopolies over their subjects. Indeed, the defeat of this stronghold will not be accomplished by intellect, might, power, a good sense of humor, or fancy footwork; it can only be conquered by the Spirit.

The Zechariah passage admonishes us to rely only on God's redemptive power and not on any other means to escape our trying circumstances. I learned through brutal experience that my faith had often been misplaced; God disapproves when we place 50% of our faith in our might and power, when our faith must be based 100% on the redemptive power of His Spirit. David conquered the lion, the bear, and Goliath in the Spirit, and those miraculous victories gave him the confidence to believe that by the power of the Holy Spirit, he could always overcome impossible odds.

It is my belief and experience that Jesus is now proclaiming liberty to the financially captive. He is now opening the debt prison doors to those who are bound. Revival is at hand, so now is the time to become a dealer in hope and approach God's throne of grace with great expectation in your heart.

At this point, we need to be clear that prison is not something to be taken lightly because it's a place of despair, crushing humiliation, misery, sorrow, and dejection. When you comprehend the plight of prisoners, your heart breaks over their desperate circumstances, and you should despise their chains, and likewise, despise your chains also.

A Dealer in Contentment

Being a dealer in contentment (a state of satisfaction) is imperative for success in the marketplace. Why should you be a dealer in contentment? *Because it empowers you and gives you much-needed clout in the Game of Thrones.*

What do I mean by *a dealer in contentment*? To consciously acknowledge the many blessings you already have, become indifferent to the ups and downs of temporal blessings, live above your circumstances, and remain undefeated when the marketplace pulls the rug out from under you.

Discontentment, or expressing dissatisfaction, magnifies what is past and vilifies what is present, without regard to truth or reason. Satan will always present to us the worthless as important, the irrelevant as essential, and that which is detrimental as beneficial, with the goal of destroying us. He will distort a partial truth and make it look logical, like a good idea. Kick Satan's rubbish firmly in the trash can!

What are the key problems associated with discontentment? In his book on contentment, Leo Babauta makes some good observations as to these key issues:[171]

o   An ideal/fantasy we are clinging to;

o   Unhappiness with our true selves;

o   Lack of trust/confidence in ourselves;

o   Seeking happiness externally.

It's a good thing to learn to react well and not be swayed by the actions of others, because if we allow ourselves to be discouraged or defeated by what others do, we can easily see ourselves as victims and fall into discontentment. We can improve our reactions to the actions of others by:

o   Not taking any negative actions personally because there are a million reasons why people behave the way they do, and in most cases, it has nothing to do with you;

o   Reaffirming your worth in Christ as your exclusive value, not affected by the opinion of other people;

o   Considering the advice of Philippians 2:3: "Let nothing be done through selfish ambition or conceit, but in lowliness of mind let each esteem others better than himself." You have already checked in with yourself and realized you are good to go - now go and help the other person.

Victory is not always found in having the right circumstances or winning the gold medal; victory is achieved in living with integrity and thankfulness in all circumstances - that is why Scripture places the gold medal on an attitude of contentment and says: "Godliness with contentment is great gain." [172]

Consider for a moment the points outlined in this fact-file, which an anonymous author sent on the blessings we should acknowledge:

o   If you have food in the refrigerator, clothes on your back, a roof overhead, and a place to sleep, you are richer than 75% of the world's population.

o   If you have money in the bank, in your wallet, and spare change in a dish, you are among the top 8% of the world's wealthy.

o   If you wake up in the morning with more health than illness, you are more blessed than the many who will not even survive the day.

o   If you can hold your head up and smile, you are not the norm; you're unique among all those in doubt and despair.

o   If you can read this book, you are more blessed than over a billion people who cannot read at all.

A dealer in contentment is someone who finds satisfaction emanating from within, despite external circumstances. Internal contentment is very rare and is the result of a heart at peace, secure in the unchanging love of God.

The Peacemakers

"Blessed are the peacemakers, for they shall be called sons of God."[173] A heart-warming portion of Scripture from the Beatitudes of Jesus.

Peacemakers display God's reconciling nature because they graciously try to repair strained relations between individuals in conflict. God honors peacemakers with the recognition of being called the 'sons of God.' What is better, a knighthood from the Queen of England or a knighthood from the King of kings? No contest, so be a dealer in peace.

Who then is qualified as a peacemaker in Jesus' sermon? First, a peacemaker takes his cue from God, the God of peace. I agree with the definition given by Tod Kennedy:[174]

"The word peacemaker is εἰρηνοποιός (*eirenopoios*), an adjective. The verb form means to make peace.

i.   The basic meaning describes one who attempts to bring reconciliation and well-being between people who are at odds.

ii. A peacemaker is one who can bridge the gap and smooth out the trouble. He can quiet the waters of the 'people storm.' This person brings peace between people.

iii. Some wrongly emphasize that this means a peace lover. A peace lover simply tries to avoid conflict."

Matthew Henry goes further with this definition and says that peacemakers generally have two attributes: having a peaceable disposition and a peaceable conversation. The former is "to have a strong and hearty affection to peace." In contrast, the latter is "to preserve the peace that it be not broken, and to recover it when it is broken to hearken to proposals of peace ourselves, and to be ready to make them to others where distance is among brethren and neighbors, to do all we can to accommodate it, and to be repairers of the breaches."[175]

There was an occasion when my father had concrete evidence that an attorney had grossly inflated his bills, which meant that the attorney stood to face heavy regulatory fines. My mother was a personal friend of his wife, and for the sake of their friendship, my father withdrew his action, but regrettably, the attorney never mended his ways. However, peace had the final say because my mother remains good friends with his wife.

As I read Scripture, peace (*shalom*) is the predominant theme of the Bible. It opens with peace in the Garden of Eden and closes with peace in eternity. In fact, we might see the course of history as a tapestry of peace. There was peace on earth in the garden, but once man sinned, peace was interrupted. The cross re-established the tapestry of peace, and in the future, Jesus will return as the Prince of Peace. He will establish a Kingdom of peace, which will catapult the world into an age of peace that will never end.

Peace is not the absence of conflict or preparation, as Matthew 10:16 tells us: "Behold, I send you out as sheep in the midst of wolves. Therefore, be wise as serpents and harmless as doves."

Being as wise as a serpent implies that you must know your enemy and understand his ways. Being as harmless as doves implies acting as a peacemaker, but that does not mean you must be passive when invaded, without defending yourself. King David sometimes went too far with war, but his son King Solomon was too passive. There will always be a tension between war and peace, but Scripture continually encourages Christians to be as shrewd as serpents but to strive for peace as best we can.

Notwithstanding all such fine attributes, I have personally discovered that by far the place of greatest power is not found by poring over balance sheets, or relying on skill and knowledge, or exerting willpower or charisma, but being a God-seeker.

The God-seekers

The term 'God-seeker' stems from King David's attitude toward God: "My soul follows close behind You; Your right hand upholds me."[176] Tommy Tenney aptly describes an attribute of a God-seeker in his wonderful book *The God Chasers*:

"Primarily, they are not interested in camping out on some dusty truth known to everyone. They are after the fresh presence of the Almighty…. If you're a God chaser, you

won't be happy to simply follow in God's tracks. You will follow them until you apprehend His presence."[177]

A God-seeker also has revelatory knowledge that true and lasting victory comes from God alone because, "Unless the LORD builds the house, they labor in vain who build it; unless the LORD guards the city, the watchman stays awake in vain."[178] That's why Kind David and Moses were always so hesitant to do anything unless they knew that the right hand of God upheld and led them.

God-seekers transcend both time and culture, and we have many examples from biblical and modern times of these types of individuals, such as: Abraham, Moses, David, Naomi, Hannah, Apostle Paul and from more modern times Matthew Henry, Charles Spurgeon, John and Charles Wesley, Mother Theresa and Billy Graham, to name only a few.

It is not the scope of this book to delve into the subject of God-seekers, but I wish to touch briefly on the three most fundamental qualities that a God-seeker should nurture, which are reading the Word, prayer, and praise (which includes worship). Now, the reader might think, "Every Christian already knows these basic virtues - so is it really necessary to revisit them?" Well, that's exactly why I'm bringing them up again: because we too often forget the very foundations of our faith. And if those foundations are not firmly in place, it could explain why your 'building' has so many cracks.

Reading the Word

The Bible is God's bread to us. Much like manna in the wilderness, you cannot store up for tomorrow or eat from what you gathered yesterday. To feed your spirit man and restore and strengthen your soul, you must eat daily from the bread of Life, the word of God, the Bible.

The more pressure you experience and the busier your days become, the more important it is for you to practice this essential spiritual discipline. Jesus said, "If you abide in Me, and My words abide in you, you will ask what you desire, and it shall be done for you."[179] It is from that place of abiding - Christ in us, and we in Him – that we will know what to ask, when to ask, and how to ask for what we need.

I have purposefully kept this topic short as readers will be all too familiar with it, though I hasten to add that during times of adversity, I tried to read the Scriptures twice a day and to spend time in prayer three times a day. Why? Because, "My soul follows close behind You; Your right hand upholds me."[180] As strange as it may seem, it's just as important to be on guard in times of prosperity, as your enemy will try to trip you up, so during prosperous seasons, you might want to increase your time in the Bible and in prayer.

Prayer

Edward M. Bounds was a world-renowned authority on prayer. Born in 1835, he was by profession an American author, attorney, and was also a member of the Methodist Episcopal Church clergy. He made this profound statement:[181]

"What the Church needs today is not more machinery or better, not new organizations or more novel methods, but men whom the Holy Ghost can use – men of prayer, men mighty in prayer. The Holy Ghost does not flow through methods, but through men. He does not come on machinery, but on men. He does not anoint plans, but men – men of prayer."

There is no better example of how and what to pray than the one given by Jesus in the Gospel of Matthew,[182] and the Gospel of Luke,[183] known the world over as the 'Lord's Prayer.' In these verses, Jesus Himself lays out the principles of successful prayer, and, if you take time to work through each line, every area of your daily life will be covered. The *Didache* from the early Church advises believers to pray this prayer thrice daily.

I love this wonderful saying: "Prayer is the slender nerve that moves the arm of omnipotence," and there is no greater truth than this. The power of prayer lies in the truth that Almighty God rules this world, and His mighty hand is forever on the rudder of human affairs. Nothing is more important to God than prayer in dealing with mankind. "Failure to pray is failure along the whole line of life."[184] He who does not pray, therefore, robs himself of God's help and limits his potential to achieve.

Prayer is how we find God's purposes for us; it is how we find God's peace, and it is a sign of our dependence and submission to Him in every area of life. Prayer was responsible for the move of God that delivered Israel from Egyptian bondage. Hannah's passionate petition for a son birthed a time of liberation from bondage and oppression for Israel that started with her son Samuel and continued through the reigns of both King David and his son King Solomon. So too, we need to be passionate in prayer if we are to succeed in imparting grace to the marketplace.

We conquer every enemy with godly wisdom. James 1:5 tells us: "If any of you lacks wisdom, let him ask of God, who gives to all liberally and without reproach, and it will be given to him." If you need wisdom, you have only to ask God for it in prayer.

I remember my pain when I fell to my knees in prayer on the banks of Lake Zurich, looking at the world's wealth around me, pleading with God to use His infinite capital resources to help our businesses and the slaves in the marketplace. I knew my prayers could move the hand of God, and all I needed was faith the size of a mustard seed. As a result, God did move miraculously in response to my prayers and praises, albeit in a very different way than I expected.

If we want our lives to be victorious, we must have a life of prayer. Praying to God should be just as natural as breathing - *our first response, and not simply a last resort.* We should be living, always before God in prayer.

Praise and Worship

If I have learned one thing about prayer, it is that it should always be accompanied by praise and thanksgiving, with worship. Praise is an act of worship. Praise can be done without actively straining to be in the presence of God, like praising God in your car, but to worship, we need to be in the presence of God.

I liked the analogy given by a man from Los Angeles, Alvin Edington Jr., on the difference between praise and worship: "Praise is lifting up, worship is bowing down. Praise applauds God for who He is, what He has done, what He is doing, and what He's gonna do. Worship is humbling before His presence in awe of His holiness and sovereignty."

Thanksgiving, which is really a 'prayer of praise,' is fundamental in making God's power available to us and through us. In the Book of Acts, Paul and Silas prayed for the deliverance of a slave girl from a spirit of divination that enabled her to tell people's fortunes. Her master made money from her demonic gift, and when they realized that their income stream had been eliminated, they gathered a mob in Philippi who attacked the two men. After being severely beaten, Paul and Silas were imprisoned with their feet in stocks. "But at midnight [they] were praying and singing hymns to God."[185] God supernaturally delivered them from jail to demonstrate His pleasure and His willingness to release His miraculous power when they gave themselves to praise and worship.

Another striking example of the power of praise as a weapon of warfare is found in 2 Chronicles 20. The event took place in about 850 B.C. and at a time when Israel and Judah were divided into two kingdoms. Jehoshaphat was the fourth King of Judah and a zealous follower of the commandments of God. At that time, the nearby kingdoms of Moab, Ammon, and the Meunites joined forces and declared war against Judah. As you can imagine, Jehoshaphat found himself in serious trouble, under attack from three nations and heavily outnumbered. However, this story is not one of defeat and devastation but of God enabling the nation of Judah to defeat the odds. God does not put such stories in the Bible just to teach us history, but *to reveal His character* and to show how we can use His weapons to defeat our own enemies.

An important lesson we can learn is that King Jehoshaphat's initial response to adversity was to turn to God before anything else: "And Jehoshaphat feared, and set himself to seek the LORD, and proclaimed a fast throughout all Judah."[186] King Jehoshaphat knew God as *Yahwah-Nissi*, which in Hebrew means: "I am the God who defends you." Literally, this means that God is your banner and He will defend you when the odds are stacked against you. His next move was to give praise a primary place by forming a company of worshippers at the head of his army, with the most dramatic results. "Now when they began to sing and to praise, the LORD set ambushes against the people of Ammon, Moab, and Mount Seir, who had come against Judah; and they were defeated."[187]

Praise prayers are powerful weapons of warfare, not only because they remind us that God is bigger than the problem we face but more importantly because: "We do not wrestle against flesh and blood, but against principalities, against powers, against the rulers of the darkness of this age, against spiritual hosts of wickedness in the heavenly places."[188] One of the titles given to the Lord Jesus is that He is the Lion of Judah. Judah means 'praise' and 'lion's roar,' so the way in which the Lion of Judah roars is through the praises of His people.

Praise is a supernatural means God uses to confound the enemy. If you have heard a lion roar at close range, you know that it literally brings you to a sudden halt with your heart beating and your body trembling because of the incredible power of the sound. It is so with praise prayers. They rip into the darkness around us, tearing down the strongholds of the enemy and releasing the light and life of God into the situation.

The Bible teaches us "in everything, give thanks."[189] So we need to learn to express gratitude to God regardless of the circumstances in which we find ourselves. We are not thanking

God for the struggle itself, but as an expression of confidence in God, who is able to work out His sovereign will and purpose for our lives, no matter what adverse circumstances we may face.

Giving thanks when you are in a place of financial need is one of the greatest challenges you will face. However, when you do so in spite of the circumstances, your praise elevates God to a place of victory over that situation, and as you hold onto Him and do His will, He will work all things out for your good in His own perfect way.

At the close of this book how fitting it is to conclude with a contemplation on the significance of praise and worship - a culmination that harmonizes with the integration of every subject into exacting sequence and position. These pages have illustrated that God will never abandon you in the marketplace, but similarly, do not neglect your sacred duty to honor Him with praise and worship for His unfailing faithfulness since He is your all in all.

All in All

There is a report written by John S. Dunne that tells of early Spanish sailors who finally reached the continent of South America after a particularly treacherous journey. When the ship sailed into the headwaters of the Amazon, an expanse of water so wide that the sailors presumed it was a continuation of the Atlantic Ocean.

Since the sailors confused the fresh water with salt water, they did not drink the water, and some sailors died of thirst. Imagine sailors dying of thirst as their ship floated on the world's largest freshwater source!

One of the deep lessons I learned during my 53-year adventure with the Lord is that He is a God of paradox; He tells us to drink the water, and we hesitate because we mistakenly presume He is advising us to drink salt water – and in the end failure to obey our paradoxical Triune God leads to our failure. The wisdom is to realize that our understanding is limited, while He sees the bigger picture, and it is our wisdom to simply obey.

Decoding the marketplace from a Christian mindset needs to keep the word 'salvation' in sight, which is defined by the word 'shalom'- the word we often connect with the greeting used in Israel, but it does indeed have a far deeper meaning - completeness in every area, with nothing missing, nothing wanting. And while the church has long limited salvation to mean saved from hell in exchange for heaven in eternity, it's time for us to expand our thinking as to the true meaning of 'salvation,' and have faith in God for things we can't even imagine.

This leads us, in conclusion, to the central theme of this book encapsulated in God's promise in Isaiah.[190] It is God's gracious gift to me, and I authored this book, so that I might inform you of this same magnificent promise—His gracious gift to you as well:

"Say to the righteous that it shall be well with them, For they shall eat the fruit of their doings."

The 'shalls' of God must be understood in their fullest depth, never restricted by our limited human perspective. This promise to 'be well' rests on God's authority and assures wellness in every situation and circumstance. If harmful marketplace codes injure you the lesson from Scripture is this – believe God more confidently than you experience or see temporarily ("the just shall live by faith"). God has and continues to bless the righteous, not those who deem themselves perfect, so that means all those who stand on the finished work of the Cross.

Carl Jung, the famous Swiss psychiatrist, was once asked by a reporter (during the latter part of his life) whether he believed in God, to which Mr Jung replied, "Oh yes, I believe". The reporter then asked whether he now still believes in God, to which question Mr Jung seemed to pause, reflect, and choose his words carefully: "difficult to answer, I know, I don't need to believe, I know."

We should learn from Mr. Jung's depth of insight. In matters of the marketplace, this book is a journey of discovery about redemption – liberated from toxic frameworks - and with righteous Job (Job 19:25) we should reach a stage where we can confidently state: "I know that my Redeemer liveth."

Decoding the marketplace begins as a research project but unfolds into the discovery of deeper, more valuable truths. Clarity of our destiny is no longer distant, for the journey has become a purposeful and prayerful path because Jesus Christ is the Yes and Amen in every Office which He bears:

your Partner, never seeking a dissolve; your Friend, sticking closer than a brother; your Shepherd, with you in the valley of adversity; your Helper, to cope with the channel valleys; your Deliverer, leading you to the sea of grace; your High Tower, as you impart grace; your Strength, your Joy, your Confidence, your all in all, therefore King of kings, and Lord of lords.

References

[1] John Edmund Haggai, '365 Things Every Successful Leader Should Know,' Harvest House Publishers 2010, Eugene, Oregon, page 188.

[2] Ephesians 4:2

[3] Extract from Dr. Martha Beck's online podcast

[4] Edmund Conway: "50 Economics ideas you really need to know," Quercus Publishing Plc 2009, page 64.

[5] Bob Sorge, 'Opened from the Inside: Taking the Stronghold of Zion,' Oasis House 2010 – www.oasishouse.net.

[6] Edmund Conway: "50 Economics ideas you really need to know," Quercus Publishing Plc 2009, page 62.

[7] Edmund Conway: "50 Economics ideas you really need to know," Quercus Publishing Plc 2009.

[8] John Maynard Keynes (1983-1946), a British economist whose ideas have fundamentally affected the theory and practice of modern macro-economics, and informed the economic policies of governments.

[9] Milton Friedman (1912 – 2006) was an American economist, statistician, and writer who taught at the University of Chicago for more than three decades. He was a recipient of the Nobel Memorial Prize in Economic Sciences, and is known for his research on consumption analysis, monetary history and theory, and the complexity of stabilisation policy.

[10] Martin Wolf, CBE, is a British journalist, a prolific writer on economics.

[11] Sir Thomas More (1478 – 1535), known to Roman Catholics as Saint Thomas More since 1935, was an English lawyer, social philosopher, author, statesman, and noted Renaissance humanist.

[12] 1 Timothy 6:10

[13] Matthew 6:24

[14] This was a fact proved by Johann Heinrich Lambert in 1768. He was a Swiss mathematician, physicist, philosopher and astronomer.

[15] See Tony Crilly: '50 Mathematical ideas you really need to know,' Quercus Publishing Plc 2007, page 22.

[16] See Tony Crilly: '50 Mathematical ideas you really need to know' Quercus Publishing Plc 2007, page 25.

[17] Adrian Furnham: '50 psychology ideas you really need to know,' Quercus Publishing Plc 2008.

[18] Bing Han: 'Prospect Theory and Applications in Finance,' McCombs School of Business 2010.

[19] Quoted from an article by Daniel Goleman, 'Business Intelligence' in Bloomsbury reference Book: 'Business the Ultimate Resource,' Bloomsbury Publishing Plc 2002, page xxxi.

[20] Doug Lennick & Fred Kiel, 'Moral Intelligence - Enhancing Business Performance and Leadership Success in Turbulent Times,' Pearson Education Inc. 2011, Kindle location 436.

[21] Doug Lennick & Fred Kiel, 'Moral Intelligence - Enhancing Business Performance and Leadership Success in Turbulent Times,' Pearson Education Inc. 2011, Kindle location 449.

[22] Doug Lennick & Fred Kiel, 'Moral Intelligence - Enhancing Business Performance and Leadership Success in Turbulent Times,' Pearson Education Inc. 2011, Kindle location 382.

[23] Quoted from John C. Maxwell, 'Ethics 101 – What Every Leader Should know,' Center Street 2003, page 11.

[24] Quoted from John C. Maxwell, 'Ethics 101 – What Every Leader Should know,' Center Street 2003, page 11.

[25] Extracted from www.christinespeaks.com – an article by Christine Corelli, 'Stop Selling and Start Building Relationships.'

[26] Dale Carnegie: 'How to Win Friends and Influence People,' Vermilion; New edition 2006.

[27] Kenneth Blanchard & Sheldon Bowles: 'Raving Fans: A Revolutionary Approach to Customer Service,' Harper, New Edition 2011.

[28] Reported in the Daily Mail: 'Shaking on it really helps seal the deal: Gesture can reinforce positive impressions and undo bad ones,' 21 October 2012.

[29] Douglas Fields: 'The Power of a Handshake' as posted in Huff Post Science, 11 May 2013.

[30] Olivia Fox, "The Charisma Myth," Cabane 2012 Portfolio/Penguin.

[31] Olivia Fox, "The Charisma Myth," Cabane 2012 Portfolio/Penguin.

[32] Article posted on io9.com by Joseph Calamia: 'Danger! Car Dealers Now in Possession of "Perfect Handshake" Equation,' Sept 2010 (original press release from Chevy).

[33] Matthew 10:16.

[34] Seth Godin, 'Purple Cow: Transform Your Business by Being Remarkable,' Penguin 2005.

[35] Refer to www.roomtoread.org.

[36] Helen Exley, 'A Portfolio of Business Jokes,' Exley Publications Ltd 1992.

[37] Proverbs 12:15

[38] Proverbs 3:7.

[39] Ecclesiastes 12:13.

[40] Proverbs 18:2.

[41] Proverbs 23:9.

[42] Proverbs 17:10.

[43] Proverbs 26:4.

[44] Psalm 62:8.

[45] Brian Banks, as described on his website www.brianbanks.com.

[46] NFL press release retrieved from www.nfl.com/news: Gregg Rosenthal: 'Brian Banks signs NFL contract with Atlanta Falcons.' 2013.

[47] Ebsco.com

[48] 1 Peter 2:23

[49] Genesis 37 onwards

[50] John Milton, English poet and politician, quoted in 'Apology for Smectymnuus' 1642.

[51] Romans 12:19

[52] Definition from www.thefreedictionary.com.

[53] Extracted from George, M: *Mary Queen of Scotland and the Isles,* www.goodreads.com/quotes/tag/betrayal.

[54] Mosley, I: 'Bank Money and the Betrayal of Democracy,' Our Kingdom: Power and Liberty in Britain (Conference Proceedings, *2013). Retrieved from www.opendemocracy.net/ourkingdom/ivo-mosley/bank-money-and-betrayal-of-democracy.

[55] McDonald, L.G with Patrick Robinson: 'A Colossal Failure of Common Sense: The Inside Story of the Collapse of Lehman Brothers,' Crown Publishers, New York 2009.

[56] Mayo, M: 'Exile on Wall Street: One Analysts Fight to Save the Big Banks from Themselves,' John Wiley & Sons Inc, New Jersey 2012.

[57] Admati, A. & Hellwig, M: 'The Bankers' New Clothes,' Princeton, Princeton University Press, 2013.

[58] Admati, A. & Hellwig, M: 'The Bankers' New Clothes,' Princeton, Princeton University Press, 2013.

[59] Fyodor Dostoyevsky: *The House of the Dead,* Dover Publications 2004, retrieved from www.goodreads.com

[60] Simplicity Partnership: 'True Cost of Complexity in the Banking Sector,' Simplicity Consulting Ltd, London, 2012.

[61] Prater, C: 'US Credit Card Agreements Unreadable to 4 out of 5 adults' – retrieved from creditcards.com / credit-card-news/credit-card-agreement-readability, 2010.

[62] Janice Harper, 'Mobbed! A Survival Guide to Adult Bullying and Mobbing,' 2013, Kindle location 205.

[63] Zanolli Davenport, N & Schwartz, RD & Elliott GP: 'Mobbing, Emotional Abuse in the American Workplace,' 3rd Edition, Civil Society Publishing, Ames 2005.

[64] Janice Harper, 'Mobbed! A Survival Guide to Adult Bullying and Mobbing,' 2013, Kindle location 351.

[65] Extracted from Janice Harper, 'Mobbed! A Survival Guide to Adult Bullying and Mobbing,' 2013, Kindle location 436-454.

[66] Acts 16:24-25.

[67] Quoted in Mandela, N. & The Nelson Mandela Foundation (2010). *'From Nelson Mandela by Himself: The Authorised Book of Quotations.'*

[68] Rodney J. Buchanan is a pastor at Mulberry St. United Methodist Church, USA.

[69] Psalm 73:4-7.

[70] Jeremiah 12:1.

[71] Such as Sun Wu, style name Changqing, better known as Sun Tzu or Sunzi, was an ancient Chinese military general, strategist and philosopher from the Zhou Dynasty.

[72] Sun Tzu, 'The Art of War,' Random House, Inc. 1983.

[73] American Psychological Association: December 2002, Vol. 33, No. 11.

[74] Online article by Barrett, R, 'The Importance of Values in Building a High Performance Culture,' Barret Values Centre 2010.

[75] Proverbs 2:6-12.

[76] Reference from Matthew Henry Commentary.

[77] Kay Arthur, 'When the Hurt Runs Deep – Healing and Hope for Life's Desperate Moments,' Waterbrook Press 2010.

[78] Steven Furtick, 'Greater,' Multnomah Books 2012.

[79] Jeremiah 1:19.

[80] Robert Hicks, 'How a Man Faces Adversity,' Bethany House Publishers, 1996.

[81] Psalm 16:8.

[82] Hebrews 13:5.

[83] Isaiah 55:8.

[84] 2 Chronicles 20:2.

[85] 2 Chronicles 20:6-7.

[86] Hebrews 11:6.

[87] John Newton, 'The Works of John Newton,' Edinburgh Banner of Truth 1985 – www.banneroftruth.co.uk.

[88] Jerry Bridges: 'Trusting God – Even When Life Hurts,' Navpress 2008, Kindle page 213.

[89] John 15:1.

[90] See Psalm 1:2-3.

[91] Psalm 94:12.

[92] Horatius Bonar, 'When God's Children Suffer,' New Canaan, CT: Keats Publishing, Inc. 1981.

[93] F.B Meyer, 'The Life of Joseph,' Lynnwood, WA: Emerald Books, 1995.

[94] See also, Os Hillman, 'The Upside of Adversity – Rising from the Pit to Greatness,' Regal Books, 2006.

[95] Ephesians 3:1.

[96] Ephesians 4:1.

[97] Ephesians 6:20.

[98] Jeremiah 17:9.

[99] D.K. Olukoya, 'From Adversity to Testimony,' The Battle Cry Christian Ministries, 2001.

[100] Maggie Scarf, 'Secrets, Lies, Betrayals: How the Body Holds the Secrets of a Life and How to Unlock Them,' New York: Random House, 2004.

[101] Jasmin Lee Cori, 'Healing from Trauma – A Survivor's Guide to Understanding Your Symptoms and Reclaiming Your Life,' New York: Marlowe & Company 2007.

[102] Jasmin Lee Cori, 'Healing from Trauma – A Survivor's Guide to Understanding Your Symptoms and Reclaiming Your Life,' New York: Marlowe & Company 2007.

[103] This is a paraphrase of Scaer's description of Levine's work as described in Robert C. Scaer, 'The Trauma Spectrum: Hidden Wounds and Human Resiliency,' New York: Norton 2005.

[104] Esther Giller, 'What is Psychological Trauma?' as published on www.sidran.org.

[105] www.psychologytoday.com

[106] www.justia.com – criminal law.

[107] Charles Stanley, 'The Blessings of Brokenness – Why God Allows us to go Through Hard Times,' Zondervan, 1997.

[108] Exodus 3:11.

[109] Ephesians 6:12.

[110] 'Descending into Greatness' by Bill Hybels is a great resource for this teaching.

[111] Zechariah 4:6.

[112] Charles Stanley, 'The Blessings of Brokenness – Why God Allows us to go Through Hard Times,' Zondervan, 1997.

[113] Theodore Millon & Roger Dale Davis, 'Personality Disorders in Modern Life,' John Wiley & Sons Inc. 2004.

[114] Sam Vaknin, 'Malignant Self Love – Narcissism Revisited – The Essay,' 2007 – www. Narcissistic-abuse.com.

[115] Sam Vaknin, 'Malignant Self Love – Narcissism Revisited – The Essay,' 2007 – www. Narcissistic-abuse.com.

[116] Matthew 10:16.

[117] Clive Staples Lewis, 'The Problem of Pain,' Collins Publishers, revised edition 2012.

[118] 1 Kings 19:11-12.

[119] Sermon 3121 by Charles Spurgeon on "The Necessity of Regeneration."

[120] Isaiah 30:15.

[121] Reference taken from Bob Sorge, 'Fire of Delayed Answers,' Oasis House 1996 – www.oasishouse.net.

[122] Reference taken from Bob Sorge, 'Fire of Delayed Answers,' Oasis House 1996 – www.oasishouse.net.

[123] Matthew 7:12.

[124] Confucius (551BC – 479 BC) was a Chinese teacher, editor, politician, and philosopher of the Spring and Autumn Period of Chinese history.

[125] Ben Dupré: '50 Big Ideas you really need to know' Quercus Publishing Plc 2009.

[126] Quote from www.quoteinvestigator.com

[127] Galatians 6:7.

[128] Maia Szalavitz and Bruce D. Perry: 'Born for Love: Why Empathy is Essential – and Endangered,' HarperCollins e-books 2010, Kindle page

[129] Prudentius circa 410.

[130] Robert Burns (1759-1796) was a Scottish poet and lyricist. He is widely regarded as the national poet of Scotland and is celebrated worldwide.

[131] Matthew 18:23-34.

[132] Matthew 20:1-16.

[133] Matthew 20:8-12.

[134] John 1:17.

[135] Luke 23:42.

[136] Luke 23:43.

[137] Muhammad Hāfez-e Shīrāzī, known by his pen name Hāfez, was an Iranian poet. His collected works composed of series of Persian literature are to be found in the homes of most people in Iran, Afghanistan.

[138] www.wikipedia.com.

[139] John Edmund Haggai, '365 Things Every Successful Leader Should Know,' Harvest House Publishers, Oregon 97402, 2010, page 152 – www.harvesthousepublishers.com.

[140] David Seamands, 'Perfectionism: Fraught with Fruits of Self-Destruction," in Christianity Today, 10 April 1981.

[141] Cited from Philip Yancey, 'What's so Amazing about Grace,' Zondervan 1997.

[142] John 13:35.

[143] 2 Samuel 5:20.

[144] Isaiah 61:1.

[145] Cited from Philip Yancey: 'What's so Amazing about Grace,' Zondervan 1997.

[146] As illustrated by psychologist Randy Kamen Gredinger in her blog: 'The Power of Forgiveness,' in Huffpost 20 July 2013.

[147] Matthew 5:23-24.

[148] Conclusion of report extracted from Michael LeFan: 'Being Nice – A Winner's Secret Weapon,' published by Michael LeFan 2012, pages 22-23.

[149] James A. Autry: 'Love and Profit – The Art of Caring Leadership,' William Morrow and Company, Inc. 1991, page 19.

[150] James A. Autry: 'Love and Profit – The Art of Caring Leadership,' William Morrow and Company, Inc. 1991, page 52.

[151] Oxford English Dictionary.

[152] James A. Autry: 'Love and Profit – The Art of Caring Leadership,' William Morrow and Company, Inc. 1991, page 77.

[153] Referenced from Stephen Swecker: 'Good Works! Tapping the Practical Power of Your Core Values,' Rider Green Book Publishers 2013, page 49.

[154] Referenced from Stephen Swecker: 'Good Works! Tapping the Practical Power of Your Core Values,' Rider Green Book Publishers 2013, page 51.

[155] Stephen Swecker: 'Good Works! Tapping the Practical Power of Your Core Values,' Rider Green Book Publishers 2013, pages 51-52.

[156] Romans 12:10.

[157] Jim Collins: 'Good to Great,' Random House 2001, page 21.

[158] Jim Collins: 'Good to Great,' Random House 2001, page 21.

[159] Extracted from Michael Austin: 'Ethics for Everyone,' in Psychology Today 3 July 2013.

[160] Extracted from www.forbes.com: 'Thoughts on the Business of Life.'

[161] See Proverbs 6:16-19.

[162] Hebrews 11:1.

[163] Hebrews 11.2.

[164] Matthew 14:31.

[165] See Hebrews 11.

[166] This principle is also outworked in Hosea 6:1-3.

[167] See Colossians 2:13-14.

[168] John Maxwell, 'Failing Forward – Turning Mistakes into Stepping Stones for Success,' Thomas Nelson 2000.

[169] Edward K. Rowell, '1001 Quotes, Illustrations, and Humorous Stories – for Preachers, Teachers and Writers,' Baker Publishing Group 1996.

[170] John Maxwell, 'Failing Forward – Turning Mistakes into Stepping Stones for Success,' Thomas Nelson 2000.

[171] Leo Babauta: 'The Little Book of Contentment – A guide to becoming happy with life & who you are, while getting things done.'

[172] 1 Timothy 6:6

[173] Matthew 5:9

[174] Extracted from www.spokanebiblechurch.com – Sermon by Tod Kennedy entitled 'Matthew 5:9, Beatitude 7,' 10 November 2004.

[175] Matthew Henry Commentary.

[176] Psalm 63:8.

[177] Tommy Tenney: 'The God Chasers,' Destiny Image Publishers, 1998, pg 1

[178] Psalm 127:1.

[179] John 15:7.

[180] Psalm 63:8.

[181] Edward M.Bounds, 'The Complete Collection of E.M. Bounds on Prayer.'

[182] Matthew 6:9-13.

[183] Luke 11:1-4.

[184] Edward M.Bounds, 'The Complete Collection of E.M. Bounds on Prayer.'

[185] Acts 16:25.

[186] 2 Chronicles 20:3.

[187] 2 Chronicles 20:21-22.

[188] Ephesians 6:12

[189] 1 Thessalonians 5:18.

[190] Isaiah 3:10